Ivy Global

New SAT Teacher's Guide
Edition 1.2

Resources & Explanations:

IVYGLOBAL.COM/TEACH

PASSWORD: greenbook

New SAT Teacher's Guide, Edition 1.2

This publication was written and edited by the team at Ivy Global.

Editor-in-Chief: Sarah Pike

Producers: Lloyd Min and Junho Suh

Editor: Sacha Azor

Formatting: Mark Mendola

Contributors: Stephanie Bucklin, Cathleen Childs, Corwin Henville, Natalia Cole, Nathan Létourneau, Kristin Rose, and Adam Wolsky

Proofreaders: Shavumiyaa Chandrabalan, Laurel Durning-Hammond, and Gideon Ng

Interns: WooKyung Lee and Jonathan Li

This product was developed by Ivy Global, a pioneering education company that delivers a wide range of educational services.

E-mail: publishing@ivyglobal.com
Website: http://www.ivyglobal.com

CONTENTS

Chapter 1
Introduction

SECTION 1
ABOUT THIS BOOK

Welcome teachers and tutors! This book is designed to help you prepare students for the newly redesigned SAT. It serves as a companion to Ivy Global's New SAT Guide, which provides over 900 pages of strategy and practice for students.

In this book you will find advice and strategies for teaching a group SAT class, as well as tutoring students one-on-one. With this information you will be prepared to help students reach their goals, even if you are a first-time teacher.

This book also offers detailed curriculum outlines for both classes and private tutoring. The curricula are presented in two-hour blocks, so you can customize them to suit your needs. They offer detailed lesson plans, activities, and practice for all sections of the test. There are also homework assignments to keep your students engaged and practicing between sessions.

Also, be sure to check out our website for even more information. As an owner of this guide you can access additional resources to support your teaching, such as handouts and quizzes.

> Download handouts (PDF) at:
> ivyglobal.com/teach

When used together with Ivy Global's New SAT Guide, this book will enable you to build a successful SAT class or tutoring program for your organization. To make this easier, we offer discounts for bulk orders of our New SAT Guide. You can find out more about using our materials for your program at http://ivyglobal.com/downloads/turnkey_brochure.pdf. Please email us at publishing@ivyglobal.com with any questions or for more details.

Have fun helping your students prepare for the SAT and reach their goals!

SECTION 2
INTRODUCTION TO THE NEW SAT

The SAT is a standardized test designed to measure students' abilities in three areas: reading, writing, and mathematical reasoning. The SAT is written and administered by the College Board. Many American colleges and universities require SAT scores for admission and consider these scores an important factor in judging the quality of applicants. The College Board is implementing some significant changes to the SAT in 2016.

THE DIFFERENCES BETWEEN THE CURRENT AND NEW EXAMS

The following chart summarizes the changes to the new SAT, which will be discussed in more detail below.

The Old SAT vs. The New SAT		
Category	Old SAT	New SAT
Timing	• 3 hours 45 minutes	• 3 hours 50 minutes (including the optional 50 minute Essay)
Sections	• Critical Reading • Writing (includes the Essay) • Math	• Evidenced-Based Reading and Writing • Essay (optional and separate from the Writing Test) • Math
Areas of Emphasis	• General reasoning skills • Challenging vocabulary used in limited contexts • Using logic to solve unfamiliar and abstract math problems	• Applying reasoning and knowledge to real-word situations • Using reading, writing, and math skills to analyze evidence • Vocabulary meaning and word choice in a greater range of contexts • Demonstrating core applied reasoning skills in algebra and data analysis

Question Types	• 161 multiple choice • 10 grid-in	• 141 multiple choice • 12 grid-in
Answer Choices	• 5 answer choices (A to E) for m/c questions	• 4 answer choices (A to D) for m/c questions
Penalty	• Guessing penalty: quarter-point deduction for wrong answers	• No penalty for wrong answers
Scoring	• Total scaled score from 600 to 2400, comprised of area scores from 200-800 in Critical Reading, Mathematics, and Writing • Essay score factored into Writing scaled score	• Total scaled score from 400 to 1600, comprised of area scores from 200-800 in Math and in Evidence-Based Reading and Writing • Essay score reported separately • Subscores and cross-test scores demonstrating skills in more specific areas

TIMING AND FORMAT

The new SAT will be about the same length as the old SAT: 3 hours and 50 minutes total, as opposed to 3 hours and 45 minutes for the old SAT. However, the format of the test is changing significantly. Instead of nine subsections of twenty or twenty-five minutes each, the new SAT is composed of four longer multiple-choice sections plus the optional Essay.

Each section covers a different skill-set. There is a 65-minute Reading Test, a 35-minute Writing and Language Test, and two sections for the 80-minute Math Test: a 55-minute calculator section, and a 25-minute no-calculator section. There is also a 50-minute Essay, for which students will be given four sheets of lined paper instead of the two sheets given for the old SAT.

THE SCORING SYSTEM

The following table summarizes the scoring system on the new SAT, which will be discussed in detail below.

SAT Scoring on The New SAT	
Composite Score (400 to 1600)	• Math (Area Score) + Evidenced-Based Reading and Writing (Area Score)
Area Scores (200 to 800)	• Evidenced-Based Reading and Writing • Math
Optional Essay Scores (1-4 on three domains with two graders)	• 1-4 for Reading • 1-4 for Analysis • 1-4 for Writing • Two graders • Not included in Writing Score
Test Scores (10 to 40)	• Reading Test • Writing Test • Math Test
Cross-test Scores	• Analysis in Social Studies • Analysis in Science
Sub-scores	• Command of Evidence (Reading and Writing) • Relevant Words in Context (Reading and Writing) • Standard English Conventions (Writing) • Expression of Ideas (Writing) • Heart of Algebra (Math) • Problem Solving and Data Analysis (Math) • Passport to Advanced Math (Math)

The composite score on the new SAT will be reported on a scale of 400-1600, rather than a scale of 600-2400. It is the sum of two area scores: one for Math, and one for Evidence-Based Reading and Writing. The area score for Math will be based on both the calculator and no-calculator sections. The area score for Evidence-Based Reading and Writing will be based on both the Reading test and the Writing and Language test. A separate score will be reported for the Essay.

NEW SCORES

In addition to the familiar scores, there will be a variety of new scores reported. Three test scores will be reported on a scale of 10-40. Unlike the area scores, there will be separate test scores for the Reading and Writing tests. Two cross-test scores will also be reported. These scores will be based on questions in the Social Studies and Science domains across the Math, Reading, and Writing tests. There will also be a total of seven subscores reported across all tests. These subscores will be calculated based on specific question types on the various tests.

CHANGES TO RAW SCORE CALCULATION

There will also be changes to the way that raw scores are calculated. On the new SAT, each question will have only four answer choices rather than the five on the old SAT. Selecting a correct answer on most questions will contribute one point to a student's raw score, with the exception of the Extended Reasoning question in the Math section: correct answers on each of the two parts of the Extended Reasoning question will contribute two points, for a total of four points. No points will be deducted for incorrect answers, eliminating the "guessing penalty" used on the old exam.

SCORING YOUR STUDENTS' EXAMS

Answer keys and scoring directions are provided for each exam in the New SAT Guide. If you would like to score your students' exams manually, refer to the following pages:

- Practice Test 1: Pages 878-886
- Practice Test 2: Pages 934-942

If you would like to use a scoring sheet that automatically scales your students' scores, please visit ivyglobal.com/teach.

For guidance on scoring students' essays, refer to the scoring rubric on pages 424-426, and pages 427-436 for sample essays with score breakdowns.

SECTION 3
HOW TO USE OUR BOOKS

This Teacher's Guide was designed as a companion to Ivy Global's New SAT Guide. The New SAT Guide is a comprehensive test preparation book geared to helping students ace the new 2016 SAT. It contains detailed strategies and approaches for every section of the test, and over 600 practice exercises and drills. There are also two full-length practice tests, and the equivalent of a third practice test split among the key content chapters.

USING THE CURRICULA

The teaching and tutoring curricula found later in this book outline exactly how to use the New SAT Guide to deliver effective instruction, with page references and detailed steps. Each curriculum starts by teaching the basic approach to each section. Longer curricula then work through increasingly challenging topics, and concepts that are tested less frequently. Each curriculum includes a mix of instruction and practice for all four sections: Reading, Writing, Math, and the Essay. In every class curriculum, there is one diagnostic test scheduled for every 12 hours of class.

The first curriculum outlined is 12 hours long, and provides a short crash course that will familiarize students with all sections of the SAT. You can use this curriculum outline on its own if you only have 12 teaching hours available. It also serves as the first 12 hours of all the other class curricula provided in this book.

If you wish to follow the 24-hour curriculum, first teach hours 1-12 as outlined in the 12-hour curriculum, and then follow the additional hours 13-24 provided by the 24-hour curriculum. To follow the 36-hour curriculum, you would also add on hours 25-36 from that outline. To lead an intensive course of 72 hours, follow all six curriculum outlines in order.

If you wish to lead a course of over 72 hours, you can find guidance in the Extending the Curriculum section.

The tutoring curricula follow a similar structure. The first 8-hour curriculum can be utilized on its own, or you can extend it to 12, 16, or 20 hours by simply working through the next outline of 4 hours until you reach your desired length.

CREATING YOUR OWN CURRICULUM

If you will not be using one of the provided curriculum outlines, the New SAT Guide still serves as an excellent primary textbook. We suggest that you spend some time introducing students to the test using chapter 1, and then cover the four test sections as needed using chapters 2 through 5.

We recommend that you work through the material within each chapter in the order it is presented. Each chapter is structured progressively, building on itself as it goes. For example, the Reading chapter starts with a description of the Reading Test and how to approach the passages, before exploring the nuances of each passage type and finally delving into the specifics of different question types.

One exception to this rule is when working with students who have good general mastery but struggle with particular concepts. In this case, you may wish to work more selectively through chapters, focusing only on the areas where your student needs to improve his or her skills. This is especially true for the Math section, where students may struggle only with specific topics.

PRACTICE TESTS

Once your students have a grasp of each section and some practice exercises under their belt, you can also make use of the full-length practice tests found in chapter 6. Be sure to have your students practice under realistic conditions so they are ready for test day. You can read more about simulating test conditions on pages 831-832 of the New SAT Guide.

For students seeking additional preparation, further timed practice is also recommended. Beyond the New SAT Guide, you can also make use of Ivy Global's two separate SAT Practice Test Booklets. These are included as diagnostic tests in the longer curricula in this book, and work well for supplementing any teaching or tutoring program with additional practice.

SECTION 4
TEACHING THE NEW SAT

This Teacher's Guide and Ivy Global's New SAT Guide are tailored to address the redesigned SAT that the College Board will begin administering in 2016.

If you are completely new to teaching the SAT, we suggest you take time to familiarize yourself with the test first. Read through the Introduction to the New SAT in this book in order to understand the test's composition and what topics are covered. You may also want to practice with some test questions from the New SAT Guide.

If you have experience with teaching the older version of the SAT, the points below will offer you further guidance on the key changes to the test, and how to adjust your teaching accordingly.

READING

The new Reading section no longer contains sentence completion, which required students to choose the correct words to fill in blanks in a given sentence. The College Board has also emphasized that there is less focus on obscure or rarely used vocabulary on the redesigned SAT.

As a result, the curricula provided in this book focus less on vocabulary memorization than most programs geared to the older version of the test. It is more helpful for students to learn words with multiple meanings, as well as roots, prefixes, and suffixes to help them identify any unfamiliar words. It is also important for students to learn to analyze the impact of an author's choice of words. This is covered on pages 153-158 of the Reading chapter in the New SAT Guide.

The reading passages and accompanying questions should appear fairly familiar to instructors who worked with the previous test. However, there is one entirely new passage category: each Reading section includes one passage from either America's Founding Documents, or the Great Global Conversation. There are also two science passages on every new Reading Test, as well as one science passage and one social science passage each accompanied by graphics. You can learn more about Founding Documents, science passages, and working with graphics in Section 3 of the Reading chapter in the New SAT Guide, which begins on page 73.

The reading passages and accompanying questions should appear fairly familiar to instructors who worked with the previous test. However, there is one entirely new passage category: each Reading section includes one passage from America's Founding Documents, or the Great Global Conversation. There are also two science passages on every new Reading Test, as well as related graphics accompanying certain passages. You can learn more about Founding Documents, science passages, and working with graphics in Section 3 of the Reading chapter in the New SAT Guide, which begins on page 73.

WRITING

The redesigned Writing section consists solely of passages, rather than multiple individual sentences and one passage as on the previous SAT. While there are no longer any improving sentences or identifying sentence error questions, students will still be asked to improve or edit individual phrases and sentences. These more targeted questions and grammar concepts are now simply embedded in full passages as well.

Thus, students still need to focus on grammar rules, but must also learn to work with a longer text and spot errors in context. The grammar rules tested on this section will remain largely the same, and should mostly be familiar to instructors who taught the previous version of the SAT. You can review grammar errors in Section 3 of the Writing chapter in the New SAT Guide, which begins on page 283.

There are four passages in each Writing Test. These passages test the grammar concepts previously tested in individual sentences, as well as students' ability to edit texts for clarity. Many of the broader questions about revising large sections of text will be similar to the improving paragraphs questions from the earlier SAT test. You can learn more about these question types in Section 4 of the Writing chapter in the New SAT Guide, which begins on page 335.

The Writing section will be scored together with the Reading section, to form one Evidence-Based Reading and Writing score.

MATH

The redesigned Math Test is broken into two sections: a calculator section and a no-calculator section. Thus, for the no-calculator section especially, students need to become comfortable solving problems and making simple calculations themselves.

As with the previous SAT, the Math section focuses on problem solving. On the revised SAT, this is expanded to include more questions with interesting topics, and data modeled on real-life situations. Be sure to help students focus on the math concepts being tested, rather than being distracted by the content of the questions.

Some of the topics covered on the redesigned Math Test are entirely new, such as trigonometry, complex numbers, and chords. These concepts are all covered in the New SAT Guide, particularly Section 7 in the Math chapter, which begins on page 735.

ESSAY

The redesigned SAT still includes an essay, but it is now optional. Students can choose whether or not to write the essay based on the requirements of the schools they are applying to. If students haven't finalized their list of schools, however, they should take the Essay to be safe, as this section cannot be completed at a separate time.

While the Essay is still sent out for scoring by the College Board, it does not form part of a student's Writing score. Instead, students will receive scores from 1 to 4 in three domains: Reading, Analysis, and Writing. You can find more detailed explanations of what those domains entail on pages 423-426 of the New SAT Guide.

The new essay is 50 minutes instead of 25, and is less open-ended. Students will be given a different persuasive piece of writing on every test, with the same prompt every time. The prompt asks students to describe how the author uses evidence, reasoning, and stylistic elements to make his or her argument. The prompt can be found on pages 388-390 of the New SAT Guide. Students should familiarize themselves with it so that on the day of the test, they can immediately start reading the source text.

Because students will need to respond to a highly specific writing prompt, they cannot prepare any examples or arguments beforehand. Instead, students will need to become comfortable with analyzing a written text and responding to it. There are multiple practice essay prompts and examples of how to analyze persuasive writing in the Essay chapter of the New SAT Guide, which begins on page 387.

THE GOALS OF TEST PREP
PART 1

Helping a student prepare for the SAT is different from regular classroom teaching. Test prep is not an alternative to the many complex approaches to classroom teaching, but is rather a supplementary approach. One key difference is that test prep focuses on improving performance on a particular exam in a relatively short period of time, rather than on fostering a holistic understanding of a broad subject domain. Thus, effective test prep builds on the skills that students learn in the classroom. It helps students brush up on important concepts and approach the test with confidence.

DRILLS AND MATERIALS

Content drills and review help students master key concepts that will appear on the exam. These activities mainly support the extensive work students have already done, but they can also help to address gaps in their knowledge. The drills used in SAT prep classes are similar to materials sometimes used in other settings, but they are designed to very closely mimic both the content and format of the SAT.

The materials in Ivy Global's New SAT Guide focus specifically on SAT content; if you'd like to use additional materials in your test prep class, be sure that they are relevant not only to the content domain, but also to the specific concepts tested on the SAT. The New SAT Guide covers the full range of content expected to appear on the SAT, and you should check to be sure that any additional materials relate to specific concepts discussed in that book.

APPLYING STRATEGIES

Strategy tips and instruction on the format of the exam help students to apply the skills and knowledge they already possess to the best of their abilities on exam day. Students at nearly any level can benefit from learning the basic format of the SAT and a few essential strategies. You can use your judgment to gauge what will benefit your students the most, given both their current achievement levels and how much time you will have to work with them before the exam.

You might decide that focusing on providing a student with test-taking strategies rather than reviewing content can also be the best use of limited time. Reinforcing strategy tips can be the best choice when a student has achieved adequate mastery of a concept, but still struggles under the timed conditions of the exam. It may also be a sound choice when a student has not mastered a concept, but may not have enough time to do so before the exam.

Section 5
Teaching Strategies

The following pages offer targeted advice on the best methods for teaching each section of the redesigned SAT. Combined with knowledge of the test and the curricula provided in this Teacher's Guide, these strategies will help you empower your students to reach their potential. You can also find more general teaching techniques in the Classroom Advice and Tutoring Advice sections of this book.

READING
PART 1

To help students excel on the Reading Test, you must first teach them how to approach a passage. Your students must become active readers who engage with the text and pull out main ideas. Main ideas are those that relate to the 5 w's: "who," "what," "where," "when," and "why." Students can practice active reading by circling or underlining two to three main ideas per paragraph. These are discussed in more detail on pages 35-38 of the New SAT Guide.

You can also teach your students to make a summary of each paragraph as they read. This helps students to process what they have read and feel less overwhelmed by long passages. You can find examples on pages 41-44 of the New SAT Guide.

WORKING ON PASSAGES TOGETHER

To help your students develop these skills, you can work on passages together. Read through a passage with your class or tutoring student, discussing what is important as you go. Start by suggesting what you would underline in the first paragraph. Then decide what to underline in the second paragraph together with your student or class. Gradually ask for more and more student input, so that when you reach the end of the passage your student or class is telling you what should be marked up.

Use the same approach with paragraph summaries, by suggesting summaries for the first one or two paragraphs, then asking for student input, and finally having your student or class provide their own summaries without assistance.

If you are leading a class, call on various students to share what they underlined in the passage, and what summaries they made. This will help students to learn from one another by seeing how their peers approach the same passage.

DISCUSS QUESTION TYPES

Once your students understand how to approach the passages, take time to familiarize them with the various question types they will encounter on test day. All of the question types are explained in detail in the New SAT Guide, beginning on page 108.

If your students struggle with a particular question type, take time to review it thoroughly, and encourage them to attempt multiple questions of that type for practice. Most of the question types will be repeated frequently, and some will appear with every passage. Thus, understanding them will give students a significant advantage.

ASK FOR EVIDENCE

Make sure your students understand that they are not meant to provide their opinion or personal interpretation of a passage, as they may sometimes do in English class. Because the Reading Test is multiple choice, there is only one correct answer and it must be supported by the text.

A good way to encourage students to find support for their answers in the passage is to ask them what words, lines, or sentences led them to their answer choice for each question. This reinforcement will help students adopt the habit of finding evidence in the passage. Discussing what led students to their answers can also help you understand where they have gone wrong when they answer incorrectly.

This technique is also good practice for a specific question type called Citing Textual Evidence, in the Command of Evidence category. These questions ask students to decide which line from the text best supports the answer to the previous question. Students will have to answer at least one of these questions per passage, so consistently looking for evidence is a good habit to develop. You can read more about Evidence questions on pages 131-136 in the New SAT Guide.

TIMED PRACTICE

As your students get closer to their test date, it is important for them to practice with timed Reading sections, so they learn how to pace themselves. You can have your students start by working on timed passages, and then build up to full-length sections. There are three full Reading Tests in the New SAT Guide, which start on pages 240, 839, and 893.

As the full sections take 65 minutes to complete, you may opt to do only individual passages in tutoring sessions or class, and have students complete full test sections for homework. Always take time to discuss any questions your students struggle with, and also review how they approached and marked up the passage if they missed multiple questions from one passage.

WRITING

PART 2

To help your students do their best on the Writing Test, you need to teach them to read the writing passages effectively, improve their command of key concepts in grammar, expand their vocabularies, and build their skill in recognizing contextually appropriate word choices.

WORK A PASSAGE TOGETHER

You should encourage students to approach writing passages strategically. Instead of answering questions right away, they should refer to the answer options, and "pick & skip," as outlined on pages 269-274 of the New SAT Guide.

Emphasize that students should not answer a question related to the main topic of a passage or paragraph without reading the whole relevant passage or paragraph, even if they have a good feeling about one of the options. Also be clear that even when a question appears to ask about only a few words, students should read at least the full sentence to be sure they're selecting the correct option.

You can demonstrate these strategies by working a passage with your class or student, reading together until reaching a question. When you reach a question, you can ask whether you have enough information to answer it or whether you need to keep reading. Make sure to highlight exactly what additional information you need for each question, and explain why the information is important. For this type of exercise, the objective is to work on identifying the type of error and how much context students need in order to reach the correct answer. Explain concepts students don't understand, but focus on coaching students in how to approach writing passages broadly, rather than on any specific English concept.

For each question, after selecting an answer option read the relevant portion of the passage back with your answer in place and ask your students if it makes sense. Encourage students to always check their own answers by silently re-reading in the same manner.

ENCOURAGE STUDENTS' BEST GUESSES

When you review guessing strategies for the Writing Test on pages 275-282 of the New SAT Guide, encourage students to try the strategies out. Sometimes students may know the correct answer to a question without being able to clearly articulate why the answer is correct. While your ultimate goal should be to help students understand why each option is correct or incorrect, while working towards that encourage students to always make their best guess. Don't simply verbally recommend the strategy, but have your students practice it. Recognize the value of students' work not only when they can get the correct answer, but when they can eliminate incorrect answers. There's no penalty for trying!

USE EXAMPLES

When you're explaining concepts in grammar and expression, it's important to provide a clear explanation of a rule or concept itself. However, it's also essential to provide examples. Many examples are provided through the grammar review in the New SAT Guide on pages 283-334, but you may find that you need to come up with more as you instruct the class. Use examples that focus on specific errors; examples with multiple errors might muddle things too much to be useful. Contrast correct examples with incorrect ones, and use them to illustrate key grammar concepts both when you are introducing and returning to key concepts.

Also remember that while grammar review may be dry, language is a very rich medium. When you're coming up with example sentences while explaining a concept, you can make them more engaging by making them humorous, telling a story, or writing about topics that are of interest to your students. You can also ask students to participate, either by offering their own sentences or providing settings, topics, or names for yours.

CREATE A CONTEXT FOR UNDERSTANDING

Grammar rules are complex, and many students will need to do a significant amount of grammar review to be adequately prepared for the SAT Writing Test. It can be difficult for students to memorize isolated facts, so try to create a framework for understanding when you can.

In the New SAT Guide, many explanations of grammar concepts show how errors in grammar can change or confuse the meaning of a sentence. When you're giving additional examples of basic grammar concepts and errors, try to highlight the importance of correct grammar by constructing examples so that they will sound much better when errors are corrected. Always remember to explain not only what the error is, but also how sentences should be corrected.

The New SAT Guide and the curricula in this book present concepts in order of complexity. Low-level concepts like parts of speech are covered on pages 283-288, before higher-level concepts like modifier placement on pages 317-318, which require a firm grasp of lower-level concepts. If you find that a student is struggling with a high-level concept, try to evaluate whether they've mastered the lower-level concepts that are necessary to break complex problems down into more manageable parts.

Sometimes, students might understand how to follow a rule, but be confused about why it's a rule. You should try to explain the reasons for various conventions clearly, but sometimes that's too time-consuming to be practical. In such cases, you can emphasize that the conventions tested on the SAT are just that: conventions. They won't necessarily match the way that students speak in everyday life, and sometimes the explanations of rules are more historical than logical, but students can master them if they practice consistently.

ESSAY

PART 3

ANALYZING THE SOURCE TEXT

Comprehending the source text is a crucial part of writing a successful Essay. The active reading skills you will be building with your students for the Reading Test will also be useful when working on the Essay.

However, students should focus on different things when they are approaching the source text for the Essay. Instead of having them summarize the content of paragraphs, teach students to follow the structure of the argument, marking logical terms and points of emphasis. They can use the example on pages 411-413 of the New SAT Guide as a model.

Teach students to highlight any evidence the author uses so that they can easily refer back to it while writing. They should also look for interesting rhetorical or persuasive techniques that might be worth examining at length. Students can mark up the source text with straight underlines for evidence and wavy underlines for rhetorical elements; this will make it easy to tell at a glance what's relevant for the aspect they're writing about.

In class or during tutoring, you can have students read texts and share elements they think are noteworthy in particular passages. Then you should ask them how the author uses those elements to construct his or her argument. Remind them that it's not enough just to identify these elements; students have to explain their importance to the argument overall.

Your ultimate goal should be to help students make connections between specific elements and the argument as a whole. Pages 402-414 of the New SAT Guide offer examples of what kinds of connections might be made. If a student is stumped, you can call on someone else to help or you can offer guidance.

WRITING A CLEAR ESSAY

The SAT Essay is a time to opt for clear, explicit, straight-to-the-point writing. Students should ensure they summarize their thesis statement at the end of their introduction, and use topic sentences at the start of each body paragraph. Remind your students to make claims about how the author constructs his or her argument, not to state whether they agree or disagree with the argument.

You can encourage strong writing by referring to the skills you've been teaching for the Writing Test. In particular, students should aim for cohesive paragraphs that develop a central point, so they can apply methods for thinking about paragraph cohesion and excluding extraneous sentences. Have students go over their own practice essays with the same critical eye they would apply to passages on the Writing Test to practice this skill.

BASIC STRATEGIES

The bulk of your time with students should be spent developing their analysis and writing. However, when you begin to teach the Essay, and at least once more at the end of the course, you should go over the general tips for the Essay Test found on pages 392-394 of the New SAT Guide. Also review the suggested time breakdown on page 395.

GRADING

Writing an essay is a more individual endeavor than taking a multiple-choice test. This means that writing essays for homework and in class is important not just so that students can practice, but so that they can receive personalized feedback.

Before grading the essays, you should review the College Board's rubric, explained on pages 424-426 of the New SAT Guide. You can also look over the score breakdowns for the sample essays on pages 429-436. A good rule of thumb for scoring is to ask whether the essay achieves the goal of the domain never, sometimes, most of the time, or always, with those measures corresponding to scores of 1, 2, 3, and 4, respectively. On the SAT, essays will be read by two graders whose scores will be combined and reported on a scale of 2-8 for each domain.

Assigning a numerical score is only a small part of grading your students' essays. You should also mark grammatical errors, employing the same terms used during grammar practice to reinforce learning. In addition, you should give students comments that will help them become better writers. It can be tempting to mark up everything that could be improved, but too many corrections can demoralize a student, and will probably be too overwhelming to be helpful.

Instead, pick two or three areas of improvement to highlight. Mark them within the essay, and also make them explicit in comments at the end. Keep it positive by framing these comments as advice, for example, "Next time, work on having clear topic sentences." Make sure to identify at least two things the student did well.

Also be strategic about how you word your comments. Using questions can be effective, since they will prompt students to start reaching for solutions. For example, if a student is not justifying his or her assertions either with logical development or with evidence from the text, instead of writing, "You need to justify this assertion," you can simply write, "Why?" This also gives students a quick script they can use in their own heads as they write. Just be sure to clarify what all those "why's" mean in your final comments, so students have a clear plan for improving on their next attempt.

MATH

PART 4

EVALUATING FUNDAMENTAL MATH SKILLS

Success on the SAT Math Test is achieved by finding solutions to problems quickly and correctly. You should teach your students to identify what the question is looking for, distill given information, create a strategy, and then determine the correct answer. The correct answer to most questions can be solved in many ways, so it is important to teach students to identify the most efficient path.

When teaching, it is essential to first assess the fundamental mathematical ability of your student or class. You need to make sure that your students have the necessary skills to solve SAT questions. Establishing strong fundamental skills also allows students to save time by quickly assessing and implementing efficient techniques, especially for the more complex questions on the test.

A quick way to assess students' fundamental abilities is to work through pages 503-504 of the New SAT Guide and to review the concepts that your students find challenging. This can also serve as a good warm-up and confidence builder. It is generally a good idea to review some of the more complex concepts, such as ratios, percentages, proportion, and rates, found on pages 494-497 of the New SAT Guide, and exponents and radicals, found on pages 498-499 of the New SAT Guide.

PROBLEM SOLVING STRATEGIES

Sometimes learning the best way to solve a problem is as important as finding the solution. You should encourage a methodical approach to finding a question's solution. Your students should first write down what they know in a concise manner. Then, have your students write down what the question is looking for. Your students may also find it useful to draw or redraw any important figures involved in the question.

Once they have organized all of the relevant facts, have your students propose a strategy to find the solution. Since there may be many ways to solve a problem, you can demonstrate additional strategies for each question if appropriate. Discuss with your students which strategies they find useful and why.

Depending on the strengths of your student or class, certain strategies may be more useful. Especially when working through the more complex questions, point out that getting the correct answer on the SAT does not always mean solving the question in a traditional manner. Work through pages 465-476 of the New SAT Guide and discuss various strategies that can be used to find the correct answer.

Pick some questions from the New SAT Guide on pages 477-479 to reinforce these key strategies. If necessary, work through additional problems in this section until your student or class feels comfortable with all of the strategies.

ASSESS AND WORK ON SAT SUBJECT MATERIAL

Now that your students know how to approach a question and are familiar with some strategies, use the New SAT Guide to work with them through the Heart of Algebra, Passport to Advanced Math, Problem Solving and Data Analysis, and Addition Topics subject areas of the test. The test is divided into a 20-question calculator section and a 37-question no-calculator section. Every math problem on the SAT can be solved without a calculator, but when the students are allowed to use a calculator, it can help them save time and avoid errors.

Select questions of increasing difficulty from the practice sets at the end of these sections. Have your student or class first attempt to solve them, and then work through them together. This way you can best assess the areas that need to be taught and reviewed. Always tailor your instruction to the needs of your student or class. As you teach the test material, ask your students what they find challenging and what they would like to cover.

Leave lots of room for questions and encourage the exploration of different methods of finding a solution. Serve as a guide when working through the questions together. Ask your students to determine the next step in the question, so they will formulate their own strategies. Afterward, you can talk about what was most effective.

To reinforce learning, you should summarize at the end of each section what strategy or method your class or student found most useful for tackling that subject material.

PRACTICE MATH TESTS

In order to achieve success on the SAT Math Test, repetition is very important. Once armed with math skills and strategies, it is critical that your students get practice solving timed math questions. In preparation for the test, time your students and have them work through the practice sets in the New SAT Guide, found on pages 809, 822, 852, and 866. Briefly review any subject matter that is still challenging your students.

SECTION 6
CLASSROOM ADVICE

Leading a successful SAT class that helps students raise their scores requires more than just quality content—a confident and engaging teacher is essential for success.

Whether you are a veteran instructor or gearing up to lead an SAT class for the first time, the tips below will offer you strategies and ideas for teaching the SAT curriculum laid out in this guide in a fun and effective way.

GENERAL INSTRUCTOR ADVICE
PART 1

CREATE A SUPPORTIVE ATMOSPHERE

The best way to have a productive and successful SAT class is to create a classroom environment where students are expected to work hard but also feel supported, respected, and that they are allowed to have fun.

Setting this tone begins with the very first class. Introduce yourself, and work to get a sense for who your students are. Students are understandably often quite reserved during the first session, so it's your job as an instructor to be friendly and personable to make them feel comfortable.

Have the students introduce themselves to the class briefly, by stating their name, grade, school, and something silly like the celebrity they detest the most, or what food they could eat forever. Fun questions like this will help to break the tension.

You could also have your students quickly fill out a questionnaire composed of questions to help you figure out how to tailor your future sessions to their needs. These questions might include:

- Do you have friends who are also preparing for the SAT?
- Have you taken SAT prep classes in the past? Which classes? What were your impressions of those classes? What did you learn?
- Have you taken the SAT before? What was your score?
- Which section of the SAT do you find most difficult?
- How much time each night can you devote to the SAT?

If a student is disrupting the class, deal with the problem immediately. Talk to the student one-on-one, either before or after class, or during a break, away from other students. If the student does not react well or does not begin to change his or her behavior, you may choose to discuss the issue with a supervisor at your company or school.

ENCOURAGE MISTAKES

Another way to foster a positive classroom environment is to let students know that mistakes are necessary, and even encouraged! Making mistakes is an essential part of learning and getting better at the SAT. In fact, mistakes are really opportunities to identify problem areas and shore them up before the test; making a mistake in practice often means gaining a point on a future test!

If students have less fear of being judged for making a mistake, they will be more open to learning new information and less hesitant to ask for clarification when they do not understand.

You can let students know that this policy applies to you too—even as an instructor, you may make mistakes or have new things to learn. If you are unsure how to answer a question a student asks you, tell your student you'll get back to him or her with the answer at the beginning of the next session. Don't waste time trying to figure it out or looking up the relevant information unless you're absolutely confident you can do so quickly. If you don't dwell on it, he or she won't either.

ALWAYS PREPARE

Always review the material you will be covering in class before you teach so that you are prepared. Knowing what you are going to cover during class will save you from feeling frazzled, and will make sure the content is fresh in your mind.

Because this Teacher's Guide provides you with your full curriculum for every class session, preparation becomes easy! Use the appropriate hour(s) of the outlined curricula to see what you will be covering in each session. You can even practice material before you teach it for the first time, so you can move through it smoothly and be ready to answer any student questions that may crop up.

Reviewing what you will cover in class also allows you to ensure you have any handouts, quizzes, or diagnostic tests you need printed and ready for your students. You can even tab the pages of the New SAT Guide you will be using, so that they are easy to find during class.

LEARN STUDENTS' NAMES

Do your best to learn your students' names quickly, ideally during the first class session. This helps to establish a friendly rapport and communicates to your students that you recognize and care about them as individuals.

Review your class list before the first session so you can more quickly match faces to names. Ask students if you are pronouncing their names correctly, or if they prefer to go by a different name than what was entered on your class list. You can also use part of your time while proctoring the first diagnostic test to draw up a seating chart or memorize names!

When introducing yourself and learning your students' names, also state how you would like your students to address you, especially if you have not met them before. Note that most younger students are more comfortable addressing an instructor by her or his last name, and this may also help to establish your authority in class.

CALL ON STUDENTS

Try to call on a variety of students during every class session. This is another reason that learning names quickly is helpful!

In order to get better at the SAT, students need to practice, not just watch you solve problems and describe strategies. It is possible that if you ask for volunteers to answer a question nobody will volunteer, or the same student(s) will answer every time. This can also make it hard to gauge how much the rest of the class understands. By answering your questions and interacting, students will be more engaged and will thus learn more.

If a student doesn't know the answer you can try to help them reach it if you sense they are close, call on another student, or pause to review the strategy or content if appropriate. Your goal is to never let a student feel uncomfortable or embarrassed because of their inability to answer. Instead, use the moment as an opportunity to clarify what is being covered and to ensure that everyone in the class understands.

ENCOURAGE QUESTIONS

In addition to calling on students, frequently ask your class if they have any questions, or if there are any ideas or concepts you can review or explain more clearly. Encourage students to raise their hands if they have a question during class by letting them know that when one person wants to review a concept it usually means several students are struggling with the same thing.

If a student is frequently asking questions that are too remedial to warrant class time, consider speaking to him or her privately to offer support and see what concepts are causing him or her difficulty.

If you sense students are extremely shy or unwillingly to ask to review certain topics, you can also allow them to submit questions or requests for homework review to you directly via written notes or even email. However, this should be a last resort, as it is far better to create an open and relaxed atmosphere in class so that students can pose questions as they arise.

TAKE FREQUENT BREAKS

Because your students will be working hard on challenging material during class, it is important to incorporate frequent breaks so they stay fresh and focused. Breaks allow students to use the restroom, stretch their legs, or have a snack. They also prevent students from leaving or losing focus in the middle of a lesson.

A good rule of thumb is to provide students with a 5-minute break every hour, or whenever you sense your students are getting tired and losing focus. This may depend on the age of your students; sophomores should be able to concentrate and work productively for longer stretches than students in 8th or 9th grade.

The frequency of breaks may also depend on the length of your class sessions, as students will likely need more breaks during a 4-hour class session than during a 2-hour one. There are 10 minutes allocated for break time in every two-hour curriculum segment, so you should have plenty of flexibility to provide breaks as will best fulfill the needs of your class.

BREAK PROBLEMS DOWN

When calling on students or working through questions together as a class, break problems down into smaller steps. This reinforces the appropriate process students should use for the question at hand, and makes challenging problems seem more approachable.

This also allows you to engage a larger number of students at once, by asking different students about different steps. For example, if you are tackling a word problem in math you might ask one student to decide on what variables should be used, ask another to generate the equations, and ask a third student to combine the equations or substitute one variable for another in order to solve the equation.

If you sense a student is struggling with a certain topic, you can ask them to describe an earlier or easier step to increase their confidence. If you ask students to read something aloud, do not then ask them to answer a question. It is difficult for students to absorb information fully when they are focused on projecting their voice to the class.

ADAPT TO YOUR CLASS SIZE

You may wish to adapt your teaching style depending on the size of your class. Generally, a small class allows for more discussion and more personalized attention for each student. You may be able to have the whole class work on solving a problem together, or be able to check in with individual students as the class is working silently.

If your class is very small—4 students or fewer—you may also be able to employ some of the techniques usually reserved for private tutoring. You can refer to the *Tutoring Advice* section of this book for more information.

When teaching a medium or large class, you can have students work in pairs or small groups to help recreate the more collaborative environment of a small class. This provides students with the benefits of teamwork, without creating chaos when numerous students try to work together.

Ideally, you can pair up students with different skills so they can teach and learn from each other. You can determine a student's strengths and weaknesses from their diagnostic test and what you observe in class. If you find it difficult to keep track of students' strengths and weaknesses in a large class, you may wish to make notes on a confidential seating chart or other document that you can refer to.

Medium and large classes are also great settings in which to integrate team-based competition. This can be used for Vocabulary Review, as discussed below, or when attempting practice questions. You can have students work individually, in pairs, or in teams to solve problems, and award points to the first student or group to explain how they reached the correct answer.

If your class is very large—15 students or more—your company or school may offer you a teaching assistant to help manage the classroom and provide more individualized attention to students. Also be sure to allocate extra time for marking any essays and diagnostic tests when teaching a large class.

MOTIVATE YOUR STUDENTS

The best way to motivate your students is to maintain a supportive atmosphere, as discussed above. However, these additional tips will help inspire your students to keep working hard.

Early in the course, help your students create realistic goals about the improvements they would like to make. Be sure to ask the students to think about why these goals are important to them, as this will keep them committed to their goals even when they encounter setbacks. They can visualize getting in to one of their top-choice schools, winning a scholarship, or simply having the SAT behind them after only one try!

Remind your students frequently of the progress they have made. This can involve looking at their improving diagnostic, essay, or quiz scores over time. However, students can also measure their progress in other ways. Remind students of all the new math or grammar content they know, or congratulate them on writing more during the 50-minute essay. Students should also be recognized for becoming more comfortable with the test over time, and developing a plan of action and positive attitude to tackle the SAT.

Finally, motivate your students by helping them to see the SAT as an opportunity, rather than a hurdle. Many students see the SAT as something they must do in order to apply to college. Instead, help them to see it as a chance to demonstrate how much they have learned in high school and how hard they can work when committed to a task.

VOCABULARY REVIEW
PART 2

There is time provided during many class sessions to review vocabulary words, roots, prefixes, and suffixes with students. Here are some ideas to make vocabulary review more fun and effective for your class.

ORAL QUIZZES

A quick and easy way to test students is to call out a word or word part and ask students to raise their hand to provide the definition or meaning. This allows you to cover a lot of words or word parts quickly, and with the entire class at once.

Because it requires active participation, this method tends to reenergize students if they are tired or unfocused. In the class curricula, Vocabulary Review is usually listed as the second item to cover in class, but you can choose to instead conduct it partway through the class to break up other material, or whenever you notice students are fading.

WRITTEN QUIZZES

There are written vocabulary, root, and prefix quizzes included with this Teacher's Guide that you can distribute to students in order to test them individually.

Download quizzes (PDF) at:

ivyglobal.com/teach

You can also create your own written quizzes, or have students complete their own by writing words, roots, prefixes, or suffixes on the board and asking students to write their definitions on a piece of paper.

You can then go over these quizzes in class, by having students either mark their own work or swap with a classmate. If a lot of students struggle with a particular word or word part consider trying to use it in context throughout the rest of the class, or quizzing students on it informally during the next class session.

TEAM COMPETITION

One of the most exciting and effective ways to encourage students to improve their vocabulary is to have them compete in teams. You can conduct this as an oral quiz as discussed above, where the first team to raise their hands gets to provide the definition. You can also provide words or word parts to be defined to each team in turn. If a team answers incorrectly, you can also give an opposing team the chance to "steal" their point by providing the correct definition.

You can alternatively give teams time to write sentences using vocabulary words. The sentences must demonstrate understanding of the definition and be used correctly, and you can offer bonus points for creativity.

It is up to you and your company or school if you wish to offer actual prizes for the winning team, or just bragging rights. You may decide that the winning team will get study aids or promotional items from your company—perhaps pencils, water bottles, or t-shirts with your company or school's logo.

You could also offer that the winning team gets to choose a snack that will be provided during the breaks of the next diagnostic test (being sure to ask about any food allergies). Be sure to keep the teams evenly matched, and to re-set the score board every few classes or after each diagnostic test if you will be offering prizes.

OUTSIDE OF CLASS

You can also encourage students to keep building their vocabulary organically outside of class. They can do this by consistently reading challenging material, noting any words they don't know, and then looking them up afterwards. This will allow them to build their own personalized vocabulary list that they should review frequently.

Students can also use websites such as www.freerice.com, which provides free vocabulary quizzes and donates rice to the World Food Program for every correct response. Older students or those with their own smart phones can also make use of vocabulary-improving apps such as Vocabulary.com or PowerVocab. Note that these approaches should be considered a supplement to their vocabulary homework during class, rather than a substitute.

HOMEWORK REVIEW
PART 3

There are 5 minutes provided in every two-hour curriculum segment for reviewing homework with your class. Depending on what homework was assigned and the needs of your class, here are some ideas for how to make the best use of this time.

REVIEW DIFFICULT QUESTIONS

Your first priority when reviewing homework should be to go over any questions that students struggled with. Ask for students to list which questions they would like to review, and cover those that posed trouble for the majority of the class. If you notice that many students struggled with a particular question or type of question, consider reviewing the relevant content.

If you sense that students are struggling but are hesitant to nominate questions for review, ask that every student in the class offer at least one question they would like to go over as a class. Note that even if students got the right answer to a question they may still be able to learn a more efficient way to answer it, especially in math. As mentioned above, if your students are very shy you can also have them submit their questions to you in a note or email. You can also send around a piece of lined paper for students to write down the questions they would like to review.

Due to time constraints, it may not be possible to cover every single question posed by students. Do your best to cover the questions that were the most highly requested. If only one student asks to go over a certain question, you can also try to work with that student individually during a break or after class to offer guidance. Another option is to check in with individual students as the class is working silently, as mentioned above.

QUIZ STUDENTS

If the assigned homework involved reading new content or strategies in the New SAT Guide, you can also quiz your students on what they read. This reinforces new material in students' minds and ensures they fully understand what they have read.

This is also a good tactic for making sure that students are not forgetting things they have previously learned in the course. For example, if you are going over a reading passage you could ask your students what steps they should be taking as they read. Some may have stopped employing strategies they learned about earlier, such as summarizing or marking up their passages. Reinforcing relevant processes often helps students who are getting things wrong understand what they missed and reintegrate that step in their approach.

ASK ADDITIONAL QUESTIONS

To deepen your students' understanding, you can also ask additional questions about the homework. For example, when going over reading passages you might ask students about the summaries they made, any words they underlined, or how they would characterize the relationship between two paired passages. For essays, you could ask students about how they analyzed the prompt they responded to.

This can also involve asking students to explain how or why they reached a certain response, which will provide an opportunity to review relevant strategies and techniques. This also allows students to learn from one another by being exposed to a variety different problem-solving approaches. You can even invite students to come show their work on a whiteboard or chalkboard if your class has one. For math questions in particular, there may be more than one way to reach the correct response.

SECTION 7
TUTORING ADVICE

Many students opt to prepare for the SAT through private tutoring sessions rather than in a class setting. Private sessions may better fit a student's learning style, or he or she may only wish to focus on certain portions of the test.

Many of the suggestions and tips for being an effective teacher are also applicable to private tutoring, so we suggest you take time to read the section on *Classroom Advice* in this guide. However, because tutoring students are seeking a more personalized learning experience, you will also need some new strategies. The tips below will help you to make the most of your tutoring sessions and fuel your students' progress.

GET TO KNOW YOUR STUDENT
PART 1

Building a positive relationship with your tutoring student is essential for motivating him or her and helping him or her work productively. The more you know about your students' strengths, weaknesses, goals, and even outside interests, the more your can customize your sessions to fit their needs.

ASK QUESTIONS

During the first session, take time to get to know your new student. Students are usually quite reserved during the first session, and understandably so. It's your job to be personable and inquisitive. Ask any questions that might help you figure out how to engage with your student and best construct your future sessions. These questions might include:

- Do you have friends who are also preparing for the SAT?
- What school do you go to? Do you like it?
- How many tutoring sessions have you signed up for?
- Have you done any SAT prep in the past? What kind? What study material did you use? What did you learn?
- Have you taken the SAT before? What was your score?
- Which section of the SAT do you find most difficult? What are your goals?
- How much time each night can you devote to the SAT?
- What are your interests outside of school?

Knowing the answers to these questions will help your student feel that you care about him or her and his or her progress. It was also help you tailor your sessions, and even provide more relevant examples. For example, if you know your student is a hockey player or loves reading Hemingway, use ideas from these sources to explain concepts and keep your student engaged.

Customize the Curriculum
Part 2

The tutoring curricula provided in this guide are meant to offer you an outline to use when working with individual students or small groups. It is designed to cover material much more quickly than in a classroom setting, by focusing only on areas that are new or challenging for your student.

Slow Down When Necessary

While tutoring sessions generally move more quickly than classes, depending on the needs of your student you may need to work more slowly and thoroughly through certain material. This is often the case with younger students, or students who have no prior experience with the SAT or standardized tests. Feel free to stretch out the curriculum and homework schedule to be less ambitious in this case.

Challenge Your Student

Conversely, you may work with a student who is already scoring very well, is highly familiar with the test, or otherwise works very quickly. In this case, you may work through the material laid out in the curricula more rapidly. If so, you can progress to more advanced material, or spend time doing portions of full tests together and carefully reviewing mistakes or challenging questions during your sessions. You can also look to the class curricula for the longer courses for more ideas on content to cover.

Focus on Key Areas

You may also work with students who want to focus on one area in particular. In this case, you can work through mainly or only the curriculum content related to that area and skim over the other areas. For example, if you are working with a student who only needs to improve his or her math skills, simply cover the math content from the various tutoring curricula, skipping over the other sections. This means that you will likely work through much or all of the material covered in the longer guides, even if you proceed at a slower pace.

HOMEWORK

PART 3

The tutoring curricula assign more homework per session than the class curricula. Tutoring students will often spend less time with you per week than they would with a class instructor, so it is important that they make time to work on the SAT independently. By getting to know the needs of your student, you will also be able to adjust the homework as needed, so your student focuses on the areas where he or she needs the most practice.

REVIEW TOGETHER

There is also more time allotted in each tutoring session for homework review than in the classroom curricula. This is because tutoring is meant to offer more personalized assistance for students, so you should aim to work with your student on any questions or concepts that pose difficulty for him or her.

At the start of every tutoring session, review all of the previously assigned homework. Ask your student what went well, and what was more challenging. This will help you to gauge your student's progress and adjust future sessions and homework as necessary.

Take time to review any questions your student struggled with by asking him or her how he or she approached the question and where he or she got stuck. Then, work through the problem together with your student. Reinforce relevant strategies your student can use to reach the right answer, or review content your student needs to know to tackle the question.

COMPLETING PRACTICE QUESTIONS

PART 4

The tutoring curricula provide ample opportunities for students to work through practice questions during tutoring sessions, just as during classes. Personalized assistance is one of the main reasons students seek out private tutoring, so make the most of any opportunities to help students directly with practice exercises.

WORK TOGETHER

When working on practice questions, again use a personalized approach with your student. Slow down and take extra time when working through content your student finds challenging, and offer support along the way. Break difficult problems down into smaller steps, so your student can see exactly what process to use to reach the answer.

If your student is very strong in a particular area, you can also challenge him or her to work more quickly on questions of that type, or skip over some questions in favor of practicing with harder material.

ANSWER ORALLY

Depending on the questions you are working on, you can also have your student give his or her answers orally, rather than writing them down. This will allow you to move more quickly, and also to have a dialogue with your student about how he reached his or her answer. Understanding your student's thought process will help you to spot any errors in reasoning or gaps in knowledge, and remedy them as necessary.

KEEP PARENTS UPDATED
PART 5

Just as you will get to know your tutoring students better than you might students in a large class, you will likely also interact more frequently with tutoring students' parents or guardians.

COMMUNICATE FREQUENTLY

The parents of tutoring students usually want to be informed about their child's progress, so keep them updated on what you have been reviewing during sessions and what the student still needs to work on. You can discuss this briefly with parents after tutoring sessions, or send an e-mail to parents and students with the homework and an update. When appropriate, you can even ask for parents to get involved with their child's preparation, for example through practicing vocabulary words or roots.

Always be polite and courteous when talking with parents, and take their questions and concerns seriously. If you have any issues communicating with parents, seek help from your company or school so the problem can be addressed immediately.

SECTION 8
INSTRUCTOR POLICY GUIDELINES

The following guidelines offer good general rules for conduct as a tutor and class instructor. These guidelines are not exhaustive; always refer to any policies, rules, and guidelines circulated or handed out by your school or company. Use common sense and good judgment, and if you are unsure of how to handle a situation always speak with someone at your company or school.

GENERAL CONDUCT
PART 1

ARRIVE EARLY FOR YOUR SESSIONS

Always arrive at least ten minutes before the scheduled start time of your session, and reserve time to prep and set up any equipment before the session.

Be mindful that transit and traffic can be unpredictable. Factor in potential delays when travelling to work, and do not use transit delays as an excuse for arriving late. If you encounter a major issue with transit, call your office or school immediately so they can inform your students. If you are traveling to a student's home, also get in touch with the student directly to let him or her know you are on your way.

CONDUCT YOUR SESSIONS PROFESSIONALLY

Act as you would if parents were sitting in. Respect your student by adhering to the following rules during a scheduled session:

- Dress conservatively: business casual is recommended
- No personal computer browsing (YouTube, etc.) during sessions
- No eating or food during sessions
- No coffee breaks during sessions
- No texting or phone browsing during sessions
- No profane language around students, parents, or coworkers
- Do not bring alcohol or cigarettes to your sessions
- Do not leave students alone, even while they are working on problems independently

CLEAN UP AFTER EACH SESSION

Tidy up the tutoring area and place scrap paper and cups in the garbage. If you borrowed materials from your school or office, return these to the appropriate location. If you are tutoring in a student's home, be respectful of the family's space.

HAVE LESSON PLANS READY FOR THE SESSION

Students should feel that you are prepared for the session and have a general structure for what will be covered.

This should include lots of collaborative work. Having students work on problem sets independently should not make up the majority of the session.
Hands-on practice questions can be an excellent way of reinforcing new material, but always include a balance of instruction and practice during sessions to make the best use of your students' time with you.

PROVIDE FREQUENT FEEDBACK

If you wish, you can follow up after each session with a lesson summary via email. This can be drafted while students are working on problem sets, and should briefly explain what you covered, what homework you assigned, what you are planning to work on next time you meet, and any important progress to note. You can copy parents on these emails when applicable, or plan to talk to them briefly after the session. Parents like to be kept in the loop about their child's progress.

BE UNDERSTANDING AND SUPPORTIVE

When overwhelmed, intimidated, or frustrated by difficult material, students can easily lose the will to work diligently. Be encouraging and patient. Praise students for their successes, and don't harangue them for their weaknesses. Set small, manageable goals and provide positive reinforcement when those goals are met.

Keep Your Commitments

When you say you are available for a tutoring session, treat that as a commitment. Do not reschedule or cancel sessions except under emergency circumstances.

Don't Give Specific Admissions Advice

It is fine to discuss general information about test and admissions deadlines with students, as well as your own experience going through the school admissions process. However, do not advise students on their specific school choices. A student's standardized test scores do not provide enough information to say which schools might be a good fit, and discouraging advice may break a student's spirit. If you have concerns about a student's admissions goals, speak with your company or school to determine the appropriate course of action.

Student Progress Is Of Primary Importance

If you feel that a student is not progressing or improving as expected, let your school or company know so they can work with you and the parents in addressing any issues. If you suspect that a student may have learning difficulties, speak with your company or school to determine the appropriate course of action. Learning disabilities should only be diagnosed by a licensed professional; <u>never attempt to diagnose a learning disability</u> for a student.

Classroom Conduct
Part 2

If you are teaching a group class, the following additional policies apply.

Arrive Early To Set Up

Arrive <u>one hour early</u> for the first day of class and at least <u>ten minutes</u> early for each subsequent class. Keep an eye out for any lost students or parents and help direct them to the classroom.

Provide Progress Reports

You may decide to send students a summary of class exercises and homework via email after every class. You can copy parents on these emails when applicable, and keep them informed about their children's individual progress through the course. At the end of the course, send individual progress reports to each student, detailing their diagnostic exam scores and specific tips for their future study. Send these final reports no later than one week after the last day of class.

Aim For Variety In Instruction

Incorporate a balance of guided lectures, small group work, and individual practice exercises throughout the class. Notice how your students seem to be responding to various teaching methods, and move on to another activity if students seem to be bored or restless.

Involve Every Student

Ask students questions to make sure they are engaged and following along. Ask them to explain their own problem-solving processes, or share their processes with their neighbors. Use a variety of teaching methods to make sure you are reaching the learning needs of all of your students. You can make use of engaging lectures, class discussion, small group work, team-based competitions and more. If a student does not seem to want to participate, take a moment to speak with that student individually during break or after class to see how you can address his or her learning needs.

MAINTAIN A POSITIVE LEARNING ENVIRONMENT

Challenge all of your students to meet and exceed their personal goals. Make sure students know that the classroom is a supportive environment for students of all skill levels, and any attitudes that make a student feel bad about his or her progress will not be tolerated. Students should feel supported by their peers, and should never hesitate to ask a question during class or approach you for help during a break.

ADDRESS DISRUPTIVE BEHAVIOR IMMEDIATELY

If a student's behavior is disrupting the class, step in immediately to address the situation. Take the student into the hallway to talk with him or her one-on-one, and inform your school or company about the situation in order to determine an appropriate course of action.

FIRST DAY CHECKLISTS
PART 3

Use the lists below to remember some key items for your first session of teaching or tutoring.
Enjoy your first day!

FIRST TUTORING SESSION

- [ ] Pens, pencils, markers, erasers
- [ ] Calculator
- [ ] Scrap paper
- [ ] Your own New SAT Guide
- [ ] Copy of New SAT Guide for your student
- [ ] Curricula outlines for two sessions (in case work ahead)

ADDITIONAL ITEMS IF TRAVELING TO A STUDENT'S HOME

- [ ] Address and directions
- [ ] Name of student and parents
- [ ] Contact number for parents in case of delay
- [ ] Contact number for school or office in case of emergency

ADDITIONAL ITEMS FOR TEACHING A CLASS

- [ ] Class list
- [ ] Copy of New SAT Guide for each student
- [ ] Diagnostic tests (with extra copies)
- [ ] Handouts and worksheets (with extra copies)
- [ ] Any audio-visual equipment and instructions for working it
- [ ] Chalk for chalkboard or marker for whiteboard
- [ ] Spare pencils
- [ ] Spare calculators
- [ ] Water (to combat a scratchy voice)

Chapter 2
Classroom Teaching

Section 1
Classroom Syllabi

These pages contain syllabi for all the class curricula that follow. They provide a snapshot of each course that you can refer to while planning your course or teaching.

12-Hour Course

Part 1

Course Summary

Introduction to the SAT	50 minutes
1 Mini-Diagnostic Test	40 minutes
Vocabulary Intro	30 minutes
Reading Test Intro	1.75 hours
Writing Test Intro	1.75 hours
Math Test Intro	3.5 hours
Essay Intro	1.5 hours
Creating a Study Schedule	15 minutes
Homework Review	25 minutes
Breaks	1 hour
	12 hours

Materials

- New SAT Guide, 1st Edition (Ivy Global)
- New SAT Mini-Diagnostic Test #1 Booklet (Ivy Global)

Hours 1-2: Introduction & Diagnostic

Instruction Time		
Task	Materials *(All Pages in New SAT Guide)*	Time
Classroom Set-up		Before class
Introduction to the Class		5 minutes
Introduction to the SAT	Pgs. 6-20	45 minutes
Break		10 minutes
Proctor Mini-Diagnostic Test	Mini-Diagnostic Test #1	40 minutes
Introduction to Vocabulary Building	Pgs. 227-231	20 minutes
Prepare Score Report	Mini-Diagnostic Analysis Scoring Sheet	After class

Homework	
Assignment	Page(s)
Memorize the first 15 roots (to *civi*)	227-228
Memorize words 1-20	231

Hours 3-4: The Reading Test

Instruction Time		
Task	Materials *(All Pages in New SAT Guide)*	Time
Homework Review	Pgs. 227-228; 231	5 minutes
Introduction to Reading Comprehension	Pgs. 29-32	10 minutes
Reading a Passage	Pgs. 34-46	45 minutes
Break		10 minutes
Reading Questions & Selecting Answers	Pgs. 47-62	50 minutes

Homework	
Assignment	Page(s)
Complete Reading practice set	63-70
Read section and complete practice sets	95-106

Hours 5-6: The Writing Test

Instruction Time		
Task	Materials *(All Pages in New SAT Guide)*	Time
Homework Review	Pgs. 63-70; 95-106	5 minutes
Introduction to Writing	Pgs. 257-261	10 minutes
Reading the Passages	Pgs. 263-268	10 minutes
Reading Questions & Selecting Answers	Pgs. 269-282	40 minutes
Break		10 minutes
SAT Grammar	Pgs. 283-302	45 minutes

Homework	
Assignment	Page(s)
Read and complete writing practice set	303-314
Read and complete writing practice set	335-342

Hours 7-8: The Math Test

Instruction Time		
Task	Materials *(All Pages in New SAT Guide)*	Time
Homework review	Pgs. 303-314; 335-342	5 minutes
Introduction to Math	Pgs. 451-454	5 minutes
Approaching Math	Pgs. 456-481	1 hour
Break		10 minutes
Fundamental Math Review	Pgs. 482-502	40 minutes

Homework	
Assignment	Page(s)
Complete math practice set	503-507
Review previous roots and vocabulary	227-228, 231
Memorize roots 16-25 (to *locqu*)	228
Memorize words 21-40	231-232

HOURS 9-10: THE MATH TEST CONTINUED – HEART OF ALGEBRA

Instruction Time		
Task	Materials *(All Pages in New SAT Guide)*	Time
Homework Review	Pgs. 503-507; 231-232	5 minutes
Vocabulary quiz	Pgs. 227-239	10 minutes
Algebraic Expressions	Pgs. 509-514	15 minutes
Linear Equations	Pgs. 515-522	25 minutes
Break		10 minutes
Inequalities	Pgs. 523-530	20 minutes
Absolute Value	Pgs. 531-536	15 minutes
Systems of Equations & Inequalities	Pgs. 537-544	20 minutes

Homework	
Assignment	Page(s)
Complete math practice set questions #1-3, 11, 14, and 30	577-585
Review previous roots and vocabulary	228, 231
Memorize next 10 roots	228
Memorize words 21-40	232-233

HOURS 11-12: THE ESSAY + CREATING A STUDY PLAN

Instruction Time		
Task	Materials *(All Pages in New SAT Guide)*	Time
Homework Review	Pgs. 577-585 #1-3, 11, 14, 30; pgs. 228, 231-232	5 minutes
Introduction to the Essay	Pgs. 387-390	10 minutes
Approaching the Essay	Pgs. 392-400	25 minutes
Analyzing Arguments	Pgs. 415-420	25 minutes
Break		10 minutes
Rubric & Sample Essay	Pgs. 424-428; 430-432; 434-436	30 minutes
Creating a Study Schedule	Pgs. 21-23	15 minutes

Homework	
Assignment	Page(s)
Complete a 50-minute practice essay using Sample Prompt #1	437-439
Complete a study schedule	21-23

24-Hour Course

Part 2

Course Summary

1 Full Diagnostic Test	4 hours
Reading Test	1 hour 40 minutes
Writing Test	1.75 hours
Math Test	1 hour 55 minutes
Essay	1 hour 25 minutes
Vocabulary Review	15 minutes
Homework Review	20 minutes
Breaks	40 minutes
	12 hours

Materials

- New SAT Guide, 1st Edition (Ivy Global)
- New SAT Practice Test #1 Booklet (Ivy Global)

HOURS 13-14: READING PASSAGE TYPES

Instruction Time		
Task	Materials *(All Pages in New SAT Guide)*	Time
Homework Review		5 minutes
Vocabulary Quiz	Pgs. 227-239	5 minutes
Reading Passage Types	Page 72	5 minutes
Literature Passages	Pgs. 73-80	20 minutes
Science Passages	Pgs. 81-88	20 minutes
Break		10 minutes
Social Science & Historical Passages	Pgs. 89-94	20 minutes
Passages with Graphics	Pgs. 95-100	15 minutes
Paired Passages	Pgs. 100-106	20 minutes
Essay Marking	Pgs. 424-426	After class

Homework	
Assignment	Page(s)
Memorize words 41-60	232-233
Complete practice passages, aiming to complete them in under 40 minutes	240-248

HOURS 15-16: ADVANCED GRAMMAR + EXPRESSING IDEAS

Instruction Time		
Task	Materials *(All Pages in New SAT Guide)*	Time
Homework Review	Pgs. 232-233; 240-248	5 minutes
Harder Grammar Errors	Pgs. 315-319	20 minutes
Confused Words & Idioms	Pgs. 319-322	10 minutes
Grammar Error Practice	Pgs. 323-324	20 minutes
Break		10 minutes
Graphics	Pgs. 343-352	20 minutes
Organizing Ideas	Pgs. 353-358	15 minutes
Effective Language Use	Pgs. 359-366	20 minutes

Homework	
Assignment	Page(s)
Complete practice set on Expressing Ideas	367-374
Memorize roots 36-45 (to *spec*)	228-229

HOURS 17-18: HEART OF ALGEBRA

Instruction Time		
Task	Materials *(All Pages in New SAT Guide)*	Time
Homework Review	Pgs. 367-374; 228-229	5 minutes
Vocabulary Quiz	Pgs. 227-239	10 minutes
Linear Functions	Pgs. 545-550	20 minutes
Interpreting Equations	Pgs. 551-556	25 minutes
Break		10 minutes
Graphing Equations	Pgs. 557-576	20 minutes
Practice Set	Pgs. 577-586	30 minutes

Homework	
Assignment	Page(s)
Read and complete practice set on Polynomial Expressions	587-594
Memorize final 7 roots	229

HOURS 19-20: PASSPORT TO ADVANCED MATH + ANALYZING ARGUMENTS + PRACTICE ESSAY

Instruction Time		
Task	Materials (All Pages in New SAT Guide)	Time
Homework Review	Pgs. 587-594; 229	5 minutes
Factoring Polynomials	Pgs. 595-602	20 minutes
Language	Pgs. 401-405	10 minutes
Evidence	Pgs. 406-409	10 minutes
Organization & Reasoning	Pgs. 410-415	15 minutes
Break		10 minutes
Timed Practice Essay	Pgs. 440-441	50 minutes
Essay Marking	Pgs. 424-426	After class

Homework	
Assignment	Page(s)
Review strategies for all sections, and all roots and vocabulary words in anticipation of diagnostic test	

HOURS 21-24: FULL-LENGTH DIAGNOSTIC TEST

Instruction Time		
Task	Materials	Time
Proctor Diagnostic Test	Diagnostic Test #1	4 hours
Prepare Score Report	Diagnostic Analysis Scoring Sheet	After class

36-Hour Course
Part 3

Course Summary

1 Full Diagnostic Test	4 hours
Reading Test	1 hour 35 minutes
Writing Test	1 hour 35 minutes
Math Test	2 hours 10 minutes
Essay	1 hour 20 minutes
Vocabulary Review	20 minutes
Homework Review	20 minutes
Breaks	40 minutes
	12 hours

Materials

- New SAT Guide, 1st Edition (Ivy Global)
- New SAT Practice Test #2 Booklet (Ivy Global)

Hours 25-26: Reading: Understanding the Facts

Instruction Time		
Task	Materials *(All Pages in New SAT Guide)*	Time
Homework Review		5 minutes
Vocabulary Quiz	Pgs. 227-239	10 minutes
Words & Phrases in Context	Pgs. 108-114	10 minutes
Explicit & Implicit Meaning	Pgs. 115-122	15 minutes
Central Ideas & Relationships	Pgs. 123-130	20 minutes
Break		10 minutes
Evidence in a Passage	Pgs. 131-136	15 minutes
Analogical Reasoning	Pgs. 137-142	15 minutes
Understanding the Facts Practice Set	Pgs. 143-146; 150	20 minutes

Homework	
Assignment	Page(s)
Complete Understanding the Facts Practice Set	146-150
Complete the practice passage, aiming to complete it in under 15 minutes	249-250

Hours 27-28: Writing Test Review & Practice

Instruction Time		
Task	Materials *(All Pages in New SAT Guide)*	Time
Homework Review	Pgs. 146-150; 249-250	5 minutes
Vocabulary Quiz	Pgs. 227-239	10 minutes
Review Grammar Basics	Pgs. 284-302	15 minutes
Review Common Grammar Errors	Pgs. 303-314	20 minutes
Review Harder Grammar Errors	Pgs. 315-324; Confused Words & Idioms Quiz	20 minutes
Break		10 minutes
Grammar Practice Set	Pgs. 325-334	40 minutes

Homework	
Assignment	Page(s)
Complete full practice set in 35 minutes or less	375-382
Memorize prefixes 1-10 (to *extro*) on the Prefixes list; Memorize Vocabulary words 61-80	229; 233

Hours 29-30: Advanced Math Continued

Instruction Time		
Task	Materials *(All Pages in New SAT Guide)*	Time
Homework Review	Pgs. 375-382;	5 minutes
Quadratic Functions	Pgs. 611-620	25 minutes
Advanced Equations	Pgs. 621-628	20 minutes
Break		10 minutes
Applications of Functions	Pgs. 629-636	25 minutes
Passport to Advanced Math Practice Set	Pgs. 637-643; 646	35 minutes

Homework	
Assignment	Page(s)
Complete questions #21-30 in the Passport to Advanced Math Practice Set	643-646
Memorize Prefixes 11-20 (to *post*); Memorize Vocabulary words 81-100	229-230; 233-234

HOURS 31-32: PROBLEM SOLVING + ESSAY PRACTICE

Instruction Time		
Task	Materials (All Pages in New SAT Guide)	Time
Homework Review		5 minutes
Measurement and Units	Pgs. 647-656	25 minutes
Essay Structure Review	Pgs. 395-398	5 minutes
Essay Prompt Analysis	Pgs. 440-441	10 minutes
Introduction		10 minutes
Break		10 minutes
Body Paragraph 1		15 minutes
Body Paragraphs 2-4		20 minutes
Conclusion		10 minutes
Peer Revision	Pgs. 424-426	10 minutes

Homework	
Assignment	Page(s)
Read and complete practice questions on Properties of Data	657-672
Students should review the comments on their essay	
Review all strategies and content from this part of the course for diagnostic next class	

HOURS 33-36: DIAGNOSTIC TEST

Instruction Time		
Task	Materials	Time
Proctor Diagnostic Test	Diagnostic Test #2	4 hours
Prepare Score Report	Diagnostic Analysis Scoring Sheet	After class

48-HOUR COURSE

PART 4

COURSE SUMMARY

1 Full Diagnostic Test	4 hours
Reading Test	1 hour 50 minutes
Writing Test	50 minutes
Math Test	3 hours 10 minutes
Essay	50 minutes
Vocabulary quiz	25 minutes
Homework Review	20 minutes
Breaks	35 minutes
	12 hours

MATERIALS

- New SAT Guide, 1st Edition (Ivy Global)

HOURS 37-38: READING: PERSUASIVE LANGUAGE + WRITING PRACTICE

Instruction Time		
Task	Materials *(All Pages in New SAT Guide)*	Time
Homework Review		5 minutes
Analyzing Word Choice	Pgs. 152-158	15 minutes
Analyzing Text Structure	Pgs. 159-164	10 minutes
Point of View & Purpose	Pgs. 165-170	10 minutes
Analyzing Arguments	Pgs. 171-180	20 minutes
Break		10 minutes
Writing Review	Pgs. 263-280	5 minutes
Writing Practice	Pgs. 375-382	45 minutes

Homework	
Assignment	Page(s)
Complete the Persuasive Language practice set, aiming to complete in 20 minutes or less	181-188
Memorize the final 7 prefixes; Memorize Vocabulary words 101-120	230; 234-235

HOURS 39-40: READING: COMBINING IDEAS + MATH PRACTICE

Instruction Time		
Task	Materials *(All Pages in New SAT Guide)*	Time
Homework Review	Pgs. 181-188; 230; 234-235	5 minutes
Vocabulary quiz	Pgs. 227-239	15 minutes
Paired Passages	Pgs. 190-198; 101-102	20 minutes
Passages with Graphs	Pgs. 199-206; 95-96	20 minutes
Break		10 minutes
Passage Practice	Pgs. 207-210; 216	15 minutes
Math Practice Set	Pgs. 822-828	35 minutes

Homework	
Assignment	Page(s)
Finish the Combining Ideas Practice passages	211-216
Memorize the first 10 suffixes from the Suffix list (to –*ful*); Memorize Vocabulary words 121-140	230; 235

HOURS 41-42: MATH: PROBLEM SOLVING & DATA ANALYSIS CONTINUED

Instruction Time		
Task	Materials *(All Pages in New SAT Guide)*	Time
Homework Review	211-216; 230; 235	5 minutes
Vocabulary quiz	Pgs. 227-239	10 minutes
Ratios, Percentages, Proportions, and Rates	Pgs. 673-680	20 minutes
Probability and Statistics	Pgs. 681-700	40 minutes
Break		10 minutes
Modeling Data	Pgs. 701-710	20 minutes
Using Data as Evidence	Pgs. 711-718	15 minutes

Homework	
Assignment	Page(s)
Complete Using Data as Evidence practice set	718-722
Complete Problem Solving & Data Analysis practice set	723-734

HOURS 43-44: MATH PRACTICE + ESSAY PRACTICE

Instruction Time		
Task	Materials *(All Pages in New SAT Guide)*	Time
Homework Review	Pgs. 718-734	5 minutes
Math Practice	Pgs. 809-818	1 hour
Break		5 minutes
Essay Practice	Pgs. 442-443	50 minutes
Essay Marking	Pgs. 424-426	After class

Homework	
Assignment	Page(s)
Review all strategies and content from this part of the course for diagnostic next class	

HOURS 45-48: DIAGNOSTIC TEST

Instruction Time		
Task	Materials	Time
Proctor Diagnostic Test	New SAT Guide Practice Test #1 pgs. 833-877	4 hours
Prepare Score Report	Diagnostic Analysis Scoring Sheet	After class

60-Hour Course

PART 5

Course Summary

1 Full Diagnostic Test	4 hours
Reading Test	2 hours 10 minutes
Writing Test	1 hour
Math Test	2 hours 20 minutes
Essay	50 minutes
Vocabulary Review	40 minutes
Homework Review	20 minutes
Breaks	40 minutes
	12 hours

Materials

- New SAT Guide, 1st Edition (Ivy Global)
- New SAT 5 Practice Tests (Ivy Global) or Official Study Guide for the New SAT (College Board)

HOURS 49-50: READING + WRITING REVIEW AND PRACTICE

Instruction Time		
Task	Materials *(All Pages in New SAT Guide)*	Time
Homework Review		5 minutes
Vocabulary quiz	Pgs. 227-239	10 minutes
Reading Review	Pgs. 34-58	15 minutes
Reading Practice Passage	Pgs. 251-252	20 minutes
Writing Grammar Review	Pgs. 283-324; Common Grammar Errors Worksheet	15 minutes
Break		10 minutes
Writing Practice Set	Pgs. 913-920; 934	45 minutes

Homework	
Assignment	Page(s)
Complete a timed essay in 50 minutes using prompt #4	444-445

HOURS 51-52: READING PRACTICE

Instruction Time		
Task	Materials *(All Pages in New SAT Guide)*	Time
Homework Review		5 minutes
Vocabulary quiz	Pgs. 227-239	10 minutes
Reading Passage Types Review	Pgs. 72-106	15 minutes
Break		10 minutes
Reading Practice Set	Pgs. 893-905; 934	1 hour 20 minutes
Essay Marking	Pgs. 424-426	After class

Homework	
Assignment	Page(s)
Review all math concepts from previous chapters in preparation for covering new content	482-647
Memorize the remaining 9 suffixes; Memorize Vocabulary words 141-160	230; 235-236

Hours 53-54: Math: Additional Topics

Instruction Time		
Task	Materials *(All Pages in New SAT Guide)*	Time
Homework Review	Pgs. 482-647; 230; 235-236	5 minutes
Vocabulary quiz	Pgs. 227-239	10 minutes
Introductory Geometry	Pgs. 735-756	45 minutes
Break		10 minutes
Right Triangles	Pgs. 757-768	25 minutes
Radians and the Unit Circle	Pgs. 769-780	25 minutes

Homework	
Assignment	Page(s)
Complete questions #1-14 from Additional Topics practice set	797-802
Memorize Vocabulary words 161-180	236-237

Hours 55-56: Math: Additional Topics + Essay Practice

Instruction Time		
Task	Materials *(All Pages in New SAT Guide)*	Time
Homework Review	Pgs. 797-802; 236-237	5 minutes
Vocabulary quiz	Pgs. 227-239	10 minutes
Circles	Pgs. 781-790; Circles Worksheet	25 minutes
Complex Numbers	Pgs. 791-796	20 minutes
Break		10 minutes
Essay Practice	Pgs. 442-443	50 minutes
Essay Marking	Pgs. 424-426	After class

Homework	
Assignment	Page(s)
Complete questions #15-30 to finish Additional Topics practice set	803-807
Memorize Vocabulary words 181-200	237

HOURS 57-60: DIAGNOSTIC TEST

Instruction Time		
Task	Materials	Time
Proctor Diagnostic Test	Practice Test #1	4 hours
Prepare Score Report	Diagnostic Analysis Scoring Sheet	After class

72-Hour Course

Course Summary

1 Full Diagnostic Test	4 hours
Reading Test	2.5 hours
Writing Test	1 hour 25 minutes
Math Test	2 hours 5 minutes
Essay	1 hour
Homework Review	20 minutes
Breaks	40 minutes
	12 hours

Materials

- New SAT Guide, 1st Edition (Ivy Global)
- New SAT 5 Practice Tests (Ivy Global) or Official Study Guide for the New SAT (College Board)

HOURS 61-62: READING + MATH PRACTICE

Instruction Time		
Task	Materials	Time
Homework Review		5 minutes
Reading Practice	Practice Test #2	75 minutes
Break		10 minutes
No-Calculator Math Practice	Practice Test #2	30 minutes

Homework	
Assignment	Page(s)
Complete a timed 50-minute essay using the prompt from Practice Test #2	Practice Test #2

HOURS 63-64: WRITING + MATH PRACTICE

Instruction Time		
Task	Materials	Time
Homework Review	Practice Test #2 – Essay Prompt	5 minutes
Writing Practice	Practice Test #2	40 minutes
Break		10 minutes
Calculator Math Practice	Practice Test #2	65 minutes

Homework	
Assignment	Page(s)
Students can score Practice Test #2	Practice Test #2
Take time to analyze questions they could not answer or answered incorrectly in each section, identify the type of question, and review the relevant material in the New SAT Guide	For example, if students missed questions on probability, review pages 681-697. If they had problems with paired passages, review pages 101-102 and 191-194

HOURS 65-66: READING + MATH PRACTICE

Instruction Time		
Task	Materials	Time
Homework Review	Practice Test #2	5 minutes
Reading Practice	Practice Test #3	75 minutes
Break		10 minutes
No-Calculator Math Practice	Practice Test #3	30 minutes

Homework	
Assignment	Page(s)
Complete the Calculator math section from Practice Test #3, timed for 55 minutes	Practice Test #3

HOURS 67-68: ESSAY + WRITING PRACTICE

Instruction Time		
Task	Materials	Time
Homework Review	Practice Test #3	5 minutes
Essay Practice	Practice Test #3	60 minutes
Break		10 minutes
Writing Practice	Practice Test #3	45 minutes
Essay Marking	Pgs. 242-246	After Class

Homework	
Assignment	Page(s)
Review the approach/strategies for all sections, focusing on areas of difficulty. At a minimum it would be helpful to review notes taken during class, and the pages on approaching each section of the test	Reading pgs. 33-58; Writing pgs. 262-279; Essay pgs. 391-398; Math pgs. 455-476.
Students should prepare everything the way they would before they take the SAT. This includes bringing all necessary materials (appropriate pencils, calculator, snacks etc.) and having a 'dry run' of their routine for test day	

HOURS 69-72: DIAGNOSTIC TEST

Instruction Time		
Task	Materials	Time
Proctor Diagnostic Test	Practice Test #4	4 hours
Prepare Score Report	Diagnostic Analysis Scoring Sheet	After class

Section 2
12-Hour Course Curriculum

The following pages provide a 12-hour class curriculum, which you can adapt as necessary to suit the needs of your class.

HOURS 1-2
INTRODUCTION & DIAGNOSTIC

Task	Materials (All Pages in New SAT Guide)	Time
Classroom Set-up		Before class
Introduction to the Class		5 minutes
Introduction to the SAT	Pgs. 6-20	45 minutes
Break		10 minutes
Proctor Mini-Diagnostic Test	Mini-Diagnostic Test #1	40 minutes
Introduction to Vocabulary Building	Pgs. 227-231	20 minutes
Prepare Score Report	Mini-Diagnostic Analysis Scoring Sheet	After class

CLASSROOM SET-UP

1. For your first class it is a good idea to get everything ready before your students arrive. This may involve ensuring you have everything you need (chalk, computer, cables, diagnostic tests, handouts) and that you know how to work any audio-visual equipment or teaching aids you will be using. Also be sure you have your own New SAT Guide book, pens, pencils, calculator, and of course this Teacher's Guide!

2. You can also set out the books and any other materials for your students at each seat, so they are waiting for the students as they enter the classroom. This may be something you have help with from any administrators helping to run your course.

3. Take a moment to review your class list before students arrive. This will help you learn your students' names faster, and help you spot any absent students on the first day.

INTRODUCTION TO THE CLASS (5 MINUTES)

1. Take a few minutes to introduce yourself to your class, and ask them to introduce themselves, if appropriate. You can ask students to simply state their name and grade, or ask other questions about things like extracurricular interests and prior experience with the SAT or PSAT if your class is small. Your goal is to help your students feel comfortable and for you to get to know them.

2. Take time to explain any class policies such as expectations for homework, when there will be class breaks, and what materials students need to bring to class. At a minimum, students should bring their New SAT Guide, pencils, paper, and a calculator to every class session.

3. If you choose to do so, this is also the time to share the class syllabus with your students and answer any questions about it.

INTRODUCTION TO THE SAT (45 MINUTES)

1. Introduce students to the basics of the SAT test. Use pages 6-11 to explain what the SAT is and why it matters, as well as changes for the new SAT as explained on page 8. Make sure students understand the format of the new exam as detailed on page 9, as well as the new SAT scoring explained in the chart on page 10.

2. Next, use pages 12-14 to explain how to plan for taking the SAT. Make sure students understand the need to plan ahead and register early for their test date, especially if they would like to apply for Early Admission as explained on page 13.

3. Use pages 15-20 to discuss general pointers for approaching the SAT. Make sure students understand how a standardized test is different from most school exams as discussed on page 16, and the importance of managing their time effectively using the ideas on page 17. Also remind students that there is no penalty for wrong answers, and walk them through how to make an educated guess using the example on page 19.

BREAK (10 MINUTES)

1. Provide students with a break to use the bathroom, stretch their legs, or have a snack. You can divide up your break time to suit the needs of your class. A 5-minute break after every hour works well, or whenever you sense your students are getting tired and losing focus.

PROCTOR MINI-DIAGNOSTIC TEST (40 MINUTES)

1. Proctor a mini SAT diagnostic for your class. Inform your students that this is a shortened, miniature version of the SAT test they will take. It is meant to familiarize them with the kinds of material and questions they will see on the test, but is not representative of the actual test and section lengths.

2. Also let students know that while they will receive a graded Score Report after the diagnostic, this score is not meant to be predictive of their performance on the actual test. It is only meant as a general indication of their current strengths and weaknesses, and is only a starting point as they begin studying for the test.

3. Students must complete the sections in the order they are given, and can only work on one section at a time; they are not allowed to work ahead or go back to work on another section if they have extra time.

4. Let students know the order and length of the test sections they will complete. The mini-diagnostic contains shortened versions of the Reading, Math, and Writing sections. Let students know that there is no penalty for wrong answers, so they are encouraged to guess on any questions they cannot complete. Students must mark down their answers on their bubble sheets, and not just in their test booklets.

5. Make sure there is a way for students to keep track of time. If there is no easily visible clock where you are teaching, you can run a countdown timer through a projection screen or mark the time remaining on a whiteboard or chalkboard.

6. Always give your students a verbal 5-minute warning when they have 5 minutes left in the section. Say: "You now have 5 minutes left to complete this section."

7. Maintain a realistic test-taking environment by not allowing talking, eating, outside notes, or the use of any electronic devices during the test. Students may only use a calculator on the designated calculator questions of the test, #5-#10. Students may not use a calculator on questions #1-#4.

8. Be sure students complete their test with an HB or #2 pencil. Pen marks will not show up on the SAT test and students could receive no credit for their answers or essay.

Download printable answer sheets (PDF) at:
ivyglobal.com/teach

INTRODUCTION TO VOCABULARY BUILDING (20 MINUTES)

1. Discuss the importance of vocabulary to the Reading and Writing Tests using page 227. Mention how vocabulary plays a different role on the new SAT, as it is not tested directly except for questions about words used in context in Reading passages. Thus, there will be less focus during the course on memorizing individual words and more on understanding roots, prefixes, and suffixes, and on mastering other portions of the Reading and Writing Test.

2. Introduce the concepts of roots, prefixes, and suffixes, using pages 227-230. Discuss a few roots, prefixes, and suffixes and how their meaning is demonstrated by words that contain them. Emphasize that learning these word parts provides a great return on students' time investment, as it will help them to recognize lots of new words they may encounter, and thus is generally more useful and efficient than memorizing large numbers of vocabulary words.

3. Introduce students to the vocabulary list on page 231. Suggest that students learn the words by making flashcards, writing them down in sentences, or using them in conversation with family and friends. You can give examples of how some of the

vocabulary words could be used in context. Remind them that while learning vocabulary words is useful it should not be the focus of their efforts. There will be time for vocabulary review in later class sessions.

HOMEWORK

At the end of class, answer any questions and assign the homework:

Hours 1-2	
Assignment	Page(s)
Memorize the first 15 roots (to *civi*)	227-228
Memorize words 1-20	231

PREPARE SCORE REPORT (AFTER CLASS)

1. Follow the instructions on the Mini-Diagnostic Analysis Scoring Sheet to prepare a Score Report for each student. You will complete this after the class.

2. Try to have Score Reports ready to return by the next class session whenever possible. It is a good idea to return Score Reports at the end of class, rather than the beginning. This way students will stay focused on the new lesson rather than on reviewing or comparing their scores.

HOURS 3-4
THE READING TEST

Task	Materials *(All Pages in New SAT Guide)*	Time
Homework Review	Pgs. 227-228; 231	5 minutes
Introduction to Reading Comprehension	Pgs. 29-32	10 minutes
Reading a Passage	Pgs. 34-46	45 minutes
Break		10 minutes
Reading Questions & Selecting Answers	Pgs. 47-62	50 minutes

HOMEWORK REVIEW (5 MINUTES)

1. There is time included in every 2-hour lesson block for homework review. Use this time to review any questions or exercises that students had trouble with, or to quiz students on what strategies or information they read about in the New SAT Guide. See *Classroom Advice* in this guide for more ideas and information.

2. Aim to review just those questions that posed difficulty for several students. There are multiple ways to determine what questions you should review. You can ask every student to nominate one question they would like to review or ask students to call out what questions they would like to review, and make note of those which are requested by multiple students. You can also suggest reviewing any questions or drills that you anticipate being challenging for students, or that you have had students ask about in the past.

3. For questions that only posed issues for individual students, try to help the student one-on-one before or after class, or during a class break.

4. As the only previous homework was vocabulary, today's homework review can take the form of a vocabulary quiz. Spend 5 minutes quizzing your class on the roots, prefixes, and suffixes they previously learned for homework, along with words from the vocabulary list. You can call or write out roots or vocabulary words

that students must identify either individually or in teams. You can also have students compose sentences using vocabulary words, or give you examples of words that use certain roots, prefixes, and suffixes. See *Classroom Advice* for more ideas and information.

INTRODUCTION TO READING COMPREHENSION (10 MINUTES)

1. Introduce students to the content and format of the new SAT Reading Test by covering the material on pages 29-32.

2. Make sure students understand they will have 65 minutes for the entire section, and there will be 5 passages, as explained in the chart on page 31.

READING A PASSAGE (45 MINUTES)

1. Cover the material on pages 34-38 about how to read and mark up an SAT passage.

2. Then, give students 5 minutes to mark up the rest of the sample passage given on page 39. Afterwards, discuss what items students underlined while referencing the fully marked-up passage on page 40.

3. After reading about Summarizing on pages 41-42, give students 5 minutes to create summaries for the passage on pages 42-43. Afterwards, discuss students' summaries while referencing the summaries provided on page 44.

4. Then, give students 8 minutes to mark up and make summaries for the practice passage on page 45, and review their work after using the answer key on page 46.

BREAK (10 MINUTES)

READING QUESTIONS & SELECTING ANSWERS (50 MINUTES)

1. Cover the material on pages 47-49 about approaching the SAT Reading questions.

2. Then, give students 12 minutes to complete the practice exercise on pages 50-51. Discuss the answers using the answer key on page 52.

3. Next, cover the material on pages 53-58 on selecting answers.

4. Then, give students 12 minutes to complete the practice exercise on pages 58-60. Discuss the answers using the answer key on page 62.

HOMEWORK

At the end of class, answer any questions and assign the homework:

Hours 3-4	
Assignment	Page(s)
Complete Reading practice set	63-70
Read section on graphics and complete practice sets	95-106

HOURS 5-6
THE WRITING TEST

Task	Materials (All Pages in New SAT Guide)	Time
Homework Review	Pgs. 63-70; 95-106	5 minutes
Introduction to Writing	Pgs. 257-261	10 minutes
Reading the Passages	Pgs. 263-268	10 minutes
Reading Questions & Selecting Answers	Pgs. 269-282	40 minutes
Break		10 minutes
SAT Grammar	Pgs. 283-302	45 minutes

HOMEWORK REVIEW (5 MINUTES)

1. Use this time to review any questions or exercises that students had trouble with, or to quiz students on what strategies or information they read about in the New SAT Guide.

INTRODUCTION TO WRITING (10 MINUTES)

1. Introduce students to the content and format of the new SAT Writing Test by covering the material on pages 257-261.

2. Make sure students understand the different kinds of passages as listed on pages 258-259, and the way questions will be presented as illustrated on pages 259-261.

READING THE PASSAGES (10 MINUTES)

1. Cover the material on pages 263-265 on approaching Writing passages.

2. Then give students 5 minutes to answer the practice questions on page 266. Discuss the answers using the answer key on page 268.

Reading Questions & Selecting Answers (40 minutes)

1. Cover the material on pages 269-271 on approaching Writing questions.

2. Then give students 5 minutes to answer the practice questions on pages 272-273. Discuss the answers using the answer key on page 274.

3. Next, cover the material on pages 275-279 on selecting answers.

4. Then given students 8 minutes to answer the practice questions on pages 279-280. Discuss the answers using the answer key on page 282.

Break (10 minutes)

SAT Grammar (45 minutes)

1. Cover the material on pages 284-286 on parts of speech.

2. Then given students 12 minutes to answer the practice questions on pages 286-287. Discuss the answers using the answer key on page 288.

3. Next, cover the material on pages 289-299 on sentences.

4. Then give students 12 minutes to answer the practice questions on page 300. Discuss the answers using the answer key on page 302.

Homework

At the end of class, answer any questions and assign the homework:

Hours 5-6	
Assignment	Page(s)
Read and complete writing practice set	303-314
Read and complete writing practice set	335-342

Hours 7-8
The Math Test

Task	Materials (All Pages in New SAT Guide)	Time
Homework review	Pgs. 303-314; 335-342	5 minutes
Introduction to Math	Pgs. 451-454	5 minutes
Approaching Math	Pgs. 456-481	1 hour
Break		10 minutes
Fundamental Math Review	Pgs. 482-502	40 minutes

Homework Review (5 minutes)

1. Use this time to review any questions or exercises that students had trouble with, or to quiz students on what strategies or information they read about in the New SAT Guide.

Introduction to Math (5 minutes)

1. Introduce students to the content and format of the new SAT Math Test by covering the material on pages 451-454.

2. Make sure students understand the different topics covered as discussed on page 452, and the score breakdown of the calculator and no-calculator sections on page 454.

Approaching Math (1 hour)

1. Cover the material on pages 456-476 on approaching the math test and question-solving strategies. Work through the example questions on pages 465-476 together with the class, so that students can see them in action.

2. Then give students 15 minutes to complete the practice questions on pages 477-479. Discuss the answers using the answer key on pages 480-481.

BREAK (10 MINUTES)

FUNDAMENTAL MATH REVIEW (40 MINUTES)

1. Cover the material on pages 482-502 on fundamental math concepts. Make sure students understand Properties of Integers; Factors and Multiples; Operations; Fractions; Ratios, Percentages, Proportions, and Rates; Exponents; Radicals; and Scientific Notation.

2. Work through the example questions in each topic so that students can see how to use these concepts to find solutions.

HOMEWORK

If you do not have time to cover all the content in this section, assign students the remaining content for review before they attempt the questions.

At the end of class, answer any questions and assign the homework:

Hours 7-8	
Assignment	Page(s)
Complete math practice set	503-507
Review previous roots and vocabulary	227-228, 231
Memorize roots 16-25 (to *locqu*)	228
Memorize words 21-40	231-232

HOURS 9-10

THE MATH TEST CONTINUED – HEART OF ALGEBRA

Task	Materials (All Pages in New SAT Guide)	Time
Homework Review	Pgs. 503-507; 231-232	5 minutes
Vocabulary quiz	Pgs. 227-239	10 minutes
Algebraic Expressions	Pgs. 509-514	15 minutes
Linear Equations	Pgs. 515-522	25 minutes
Break		10 minutes
Inequalities	Pgs. 523-530	20 minutes
Absolute Value	Pgs. 531-536	15 minutes
Systems of Equations & Inequalities	Pgs. 537-544	20 minutes

HOMEWORK REVIEW (5 MINUTES)

1. Use this time to review any questions or exercises that students had trouble with, or to quiz students on what strategies or information they read about in the New SAT Guide.

VOCABULARY QUIZ (10 MINUTES)

1. Spend 10 minutes quizzing your class on the roots, prefixes, and suffixes they previously learned for homework, along with words from the vocabulary list. You can call or write out roots or vocabulary words that students must identify either individually or in teams. You can also have students compose sentences using vocabulary words, or give examples of words that use certain roots, prefixes, and suffixes. See *Classroom Advice* for more ideas and information.

2. You can also complete the vocabulary quiz at another point during your class session, such as halfway through, to help break up other material and provide variety.

ALGEBRAIC EXPRESSIONS (15 MINUTES)

1. Cover the material on pages 509-511 on algebraic expressions. Make sure students understand the distributive property and factoring.

2. Give students 8 minutes to complete the practice questions on pages 511-512. Discuss the answers using the answer key on page 514.

LINEAR EQUATIONS (30 MINUTES)

1. Cover the material on pages 515-520 on linear equations. Make sure students understand how to isolate a variable and work with equations with two variables.

2. Give students 8 minutes to complete the practice questions on page 520. Discuss the answers using the answer key on page 522.

BREAK (10 MINUTES)

INEQUALITIES (20 MINUTES)

1. Cover the material on pages 523-527 on inequalities. Make sure students understand the rules for when inequalities are preserved or reversed, as discussed on page 524.

2. Give students 8 minutes to complete the practice questions on pages 527-528. Discuss the answers using the answer key on page 530.

ABSOLUTE VALUE (15 MINUTES)

1. Cover the material on pages 531-534 on absolute value. Make sure students understand that an absolute value will always be a positive number or zero.

2. Give students 5 minutes to complete the practice questions on page 534-535. Discuss the answers using the answer key on page 536.

Systems of Equations & Inequalities (20 minutes)

1. Cover the material on pages 537-541 on systems of equations & inequalities. Make sure students understand the various ways a system of equations can be solved.

2. Give students 8 minutes to complete the practice questions on page 542. Discuss the answers using the answer key on page 544.

Homework

At the end of class, answer any questions and assign the homework:

Hours 9-10	
Assignment	Page(s)
Complete math practice set questions #1-3, 11, 14, and 30	577-585
Review previous roots and vocabulary	228, 231
Memorize next 10 roots	228
Memorize words 21-40	232-233

HOURS 11-12
THE ESSAY + CREATING A STUDY PLAN

Task	Materials (All Pages in New SAT Guide)	Time
Homework Review	Pgs. 577-585 #1-3, 11, 14, 30; pgs. 228, 231-232	5 minutes
Introduction to the Essay	Pgs. 387-390	10 minutes
Approaching the Essay	Pgs. 392-400	25 minutes
Analyzing Arguments	Pgs. 415-420	25 minutes
Break		10 minutes
Rubric & Sample Essay	Pgs. 424-428; 430-432; 434-436	30 minutes
Creating a Study Schedule	Pgs. 21-23	15 minutes

HOMEWORK REVIEW (5 MINUTES)

1. Use this time to review any questions or exercises that students had trouble with, or to quiz students on what strategies or information they read about in the New SAT Guide.

INTRODUCTION TO THE ESSAY (10 MINUTES)

1. Introduce students to the new format and prompt style of the SAT Essay by covering the material on pages 387-390. Make sure students understand the new standard prompt introduction, and the kind of passage they can expect to respond to.

APPROACHING THE ESSAY (25 MINUTES)

1. Cover the material on pages 392-398 on approaching the essay.

2. Then give students 15 minutes to answer the practice questions on pages 399-400. Discuss the answers as a class.

Analyzing Arguments (25 minutes)

1. Discuss the sample passage analysis on pages 415-418 so students can see what to look for in a prompt passage.

2. Then discuss the identified themes from the passage on pages 418-420, so students can see how to organize what they saw in the passage into themes they can use to write their essay.

Break (10 minutes)

Rubric & Sample Essay (30 minutes)

1. Review the College Board's Rubric on pages 424-426 to show students what their essays should contain.

2. Have students read the sample essay prompt and passage on pages 427-428.

3. Next, review Student Sample Essay #2 on page 430, and the score breakdown on pages 431-432.

4. Next, review Student Sample Essay #4 on pages 434-435, and the score breakdown on page 436. Have a discussion with students about what makes this a better essay than #2, and what edits they could make to essay #2 to receive a higher score.

Creating a Study Schedule (15 minutes)

1. Discuss the importance of creating a study schedule, using pages 21-23. You can help students begin filling in the schedule chart on page 23.

2. Encourage students to identify their own strengths and weaknesses based on their mini-diagnostic and their homework during the course. They should aim to spend more time on their weakest area, while not neglecting the others.

3. To keep moving forward on any section of the test, students can first review the content that was covered during the course by re-reading those portions of the book. Then, they should keep moving through the relevant chapter by reading the content and strategies, and completing all the practice questions and drills. Also encourage students to keep memorizing vocabulary words and roots, prefixes, and suffixes.

4. If you so choose, you can also present students with specific study suggestions or homework based on the longer course curricula provided in this manual.

5. There are full-length practice sections at the end of each chapter that students should use for practice. Encourage students to attempt these sections timed, so they will be prepared for the time pressure of the test.

6. Encourage students to practice with full-length diagnostics close to their test date. There are 2 complete tests in their New SAT Guide on pages 833-942 that students can use for this purpose. Encourage them to create a realistic test-taking environment, as described on pages 831-832. They can score the tests themselves after completing them, using the instructions that follow each test.

7. Also encourage students to read about what to expect on Test Day, including a checklist of what to bring, on pages 24-26.

HOMEWORK

At the end of class, answer any questions and assign the homework:

Hours 11-12	
Assignment	Page(s)
Complete a 50-minute practice essay using Sample Prompt #1	437-439
Complete a study schedule	21-23

SECTION 3
24-HOUR COURSE CURRICULUM

The 24-hour course consists of the following curriculum pages built on top of the previous 12-hour course. To complete the full 24-hour course, first work through hours 1-12 from the 12-hour course, and then continue with the following pages to work through hours 13-24.

HOURS 13-14
READING PASSAGE TYPES

Task	Materials (All Pages in New SAT Guide)	Time
Homework Review		5 minutes
Vocabulary Quiz	Pgs. 227-239	5 minutes
Reading Passage Types	Page 72	5 minutes
Literature Passages	Pgs. 73-80	20 minutes
Science Passages	Pgs. 81-88	20 minutes
Break		10 minutes
Social Science & Historical Passages	Pgs. 89-94	20 minutes
Passages with Graphics	Pgs. 95-100	15 minutes
Paired Passages	Pgs. 100-106	20 minutes
Essay Marking	Pgs. 424-426	After class

HOMEWORK REVIEW (5 MINUTES)

1. Use this time to review any questions or exercises that students had trouble with, or to quiz students on what strategies or information they read about in the New SAT Guide.

2. Also collect the timed 50-minute essay that students completed for homework.

VOCABULARY QUIZ (5 MINUTES)

1. Spend 5 minutes quizzing your class on the roots, prefixes, and suffixes they previously learned for homework, along with words from the vocabulary list. You can call or write out roots or vocabulary words that students must identify either individually or in teams. You can also have students compose sentences using vocabulary words, or give examples of words that use certain roots, prefixes, and suffixes. See *Classroom Advice* for more ideas and information.

2. You can also give students a written quiz to complete. As an owner of this book you can download quizzes on roots, prefixes, suffixes, and vocabulary words for your use.

Download handouts (PDF) at:

ivyglobal.com/teach

3. You can also complete the vocabulary quiz at another point during your class session, such as halfway through, to help break up other material and provide variety.

READING PASSAGE TYPES (5 MINUTES)

1. Discuss the different types of SAT Reading passages using page 72. Make sure students understand that they will always see the same types of passages on each SAT test: two Social Science passages, two Science passages, and a Literature passage.

LITERATURE PASSAGES (20 MINUTES)

1. Cover the material on pages 73-76 on Literature passages.

2. Give students 5 minutes to read, mark up, and make summaries for the literature passage on page 77. Then discuss the passage as a class, including instances of figurative language or characterization, as well as the passage structure.

3. Give students 3 minutes to complete the questions on pages 77-78. Discuss the answers using the answer key on page 80.

Science Passages (20 minutes)

1. Cover the material on pages 81-86 on Science passages. Make sure students understand the different elements of an argument, as explained in the chart on pages 82-83.

2. Give students 5 minutes to read, mark up, and make summaries for the science passage on pages 86-87. Then discuss the passage as a class, including its arguments and any experiments described.

3. Give students 3 minutes to complete the questions on page 87. Discuss the answers using the answer key on page 88.

Break (10 minutes)

Social Science & Historical Passages (20 minutes)

1. Cover the material on pages 89-91 on Social Science & Historical Passages. Make sure students understand what to expect from Founding Documents or Great Global Conversation passages, as described on page 89.

2. Give students 5 minutes to read, mark up, and make summaries for the Founding Documents passage on page 92. Then discuss the passage as a class, including any rhetorical techniques.

3. Give students 3 minutes to complete the questions on page 93. Discuss the answers using the answer key on page 94.

Passages with Graphics (15 minutes)

1. Cover the material on pages 95-96 on Passages with Graphics. Make sure students understand the common elements in graphics, as described in the chart on pages 95-96.

2. Give students 5 minutes to read, mark up, and make summaries for the passage and graphic on pages 96-98. Then discuss the graphic as a class, asking students to identify the common elements found in the graph.

3. Give students 3 minutes to complete the questions on page 98. Discuss the answers using the answer key on page 100.

PAIRED PASSAGES (20 MINUTES)

1. Cover the material on pages 101-102 on Paired Passages. Make sure students understand the many ways that passages can be related to one another.

2. Give students 5 minutes to read, mark up, and make summaries for the two passages on pages 103-104, breaking halfway through to discuss Passage 1 first. Then discuss both passages as a class, asking students to identify the similarities and differences between the passages.

3. For example, students should be able to spot that both passages discuss the different shift lengths that physicians-in-training have during their residency. Passage 1 suggests that longer shifts can be harmful to both patients and physicians, while Passage 2 instead argues that shorter shifts, and the "shift" mentality itself, are damaging to patients whose care is no longer the responsibility of one appointed doctor. Passage 1 cites evidence from various studies in its argument, while Passage 2 does not, instead explaining the implications of the various shift lengths. Both passages also discuss the new transition to team-based care, though they draw different conclusions about its effects. Passage 1 states that this is caused by increased specialty in medicine, and suggests the need for increased communication, while Passage 2 implies that this change is caused in part by committee regulations, and is detrimental to patient care.

4. Give students 3 minutes to complete the questions on page 104. Discuss the answers using the answer key on page 106.

ESSAY MARKING (AFTER CLASS)

1. Before the next class session mark each student's essay using the College Board's rubric provided on pages 424-426. Provide a score of 1-4 in each of Reading, Analysis, and Writing, with notes if applicable.

2. Provide comments on how to improve where appropriate, and indicate any relevant parts of the essay that demonstrate good work or could be edited. You may also note any issues with grammar, spelling, or diction.

HOMEWORK

At the end of class, answer any questions and assign the homework:

Hours 13-14	
Assignment	Page(s)
Memorize words 41-60	232-233
Complete practice passages, aiming to complete them in under 40 minutes	240-248

Hours 15-16

Advanced Grammar + Expressing Ideas

Task	Materials (All Pages in New SAT Guide)	Time
Homework Review	Pgs. 232-233; 240-248	5 minutes
Harder Grammar Errors	Pgs. 315-319	20 minutes
Confused Words & Idioms	Pgs. 319-322	10 minutes
Grammar Error Practice	Pgs. 323-324	20 minutes
Break		10 minutes
Graphics	Pgs. 343-352	20 minutes
Organizing Ideas	Pgs. 353-358	15 minutes
Effective Language Use	Pgs. 359-366	20 minutes

Homework Review (5 minutes)

1. Use this time to review any questions or exercises that students had trouble with, or to quiz students on what strategies or information they read about in the New SAT Guide. Explanations for some of the more challenging questions are given below.

    o #1—Look for evidence in the passage that describes DuBois' attitude. Though poor working conditions are mentioned (A), DuBois never expresses relief at having found work. Nor does he express indifference (C), or worry (B), as he instead describes the joy he feels at teaching his attentive students, making (D) the correct choice.

    o #3—Analyze the purpose of the author in drawing this parallel. The author makes no mention of (A), and likewise (B) is incorrect as the author does not discuss any particular techniques. While (C) may be tempting, as Dubois discusses the pleasures of his chase, it is a distortion of DuBois' actual point and reason for drawing the hunting parallel, reflected more accurately in (D).

o #9—While (A) is irrelevant, (C) offers reasons why students stopped attending school without addressing DuBois' reaction. (D) offers one example of DuBois' action when a particular student ceased attending class, but only (B) address DuBois' broader reaction and most directly supports the answer in #8.

o #10—Answer choices (B) and (C) might describe effects of DuBois' trek up the hill, but do not serve as replacements for "toiling." While (A) may be tempting, (D) is a better fit and more nearly matches the meaning and connotation of "toiling."

o #15—Roosevelt does not offer any statistics, so choice (D) is out. While (A), (B), and (C), are all similar, Roosevelt does not make much mention of political parties as suggested in (B), and the evidence in the passage does not support the specific references implied by answer choice (C), so answer (A) is the best choice.

o #17—Always refer back to the lines referenced in the question. Lines 8-12 repeat the word "win" four times, ending with, "Again they are in a mood to win. Again they will win." (C) is irrelevant, while (B) and (D) suggest changes that the lines themselves do not imply. Only (A) makes sense in this context.

o #22—In this question, Roosevelt references a political party whose inaction may have contributed to some of the nation's crises. The tone of (A), (C), and (D) thus do not fit with Roosevelt's message and cannot substitute for "indifferent." Only (B) captures Roosevelt's meaning.

o #24—Consider the tone of Passage 1. Since Passage 1 argues in favor of using genome sequencing, (B) is incorrect, and since the author takes a position, (D) does not make sense. The answer must thus either be (A) or (C), hinging on whether the author references the opposing perspective. Refer back to the passage. The author does mention potential mistakes in genome sequencing, as well as limits. This means (C) is incorrect and (A) is the right answer choice.

○ #25—While (B) and (C) do not support the answer to #24, both (A) and (D) discuss potential limitations of genome sequencing as well as the author's take on them. Refer back to the answer of #24: which answer choice most directly supports the idea the author is "an excited proponent"? Answer choice (D) references the "incredible science behind sequencing" while (A) only mentions that there are "not many" mistakes in this new science. Thus, the tone of the lines in choice (D) make it a stronger answer.

○ #27— This question requires you to make an inference based on the perspectives of the authors in the two passages. While (A) and (C) do not make sense given Passage 1's viewpoint, (D) is not supported by either passage. Choice (B) is the strongest choice, as the author of Passage 1 discusses likely improvements to the technology and the author of Passage 2 makes reference in the final line to the projected future progress of genome sequencing.

○ #30—Answer choice (D) does not make sense given the purpose of Passage 2, while (C) is incorrect, as the author does not specify the mutations and so is not using them as examples. While (B) may be tempting, the author does not in fact discuss whether the mutations are harmless, and it would be incorrect to assume this reading, making (A) the most accurate answer choice.

○ #38—Consider the author's praise of Shakespeare. With this in mind, (B) and (C) do not make sense, as the author directly mentions that Shakespeare was not this type of actor. While (A) may be tempting, as the author praise Shakespeare's skill in the "subtle craft of the character actor, an art of remarkable modesty and extraordinary self-restraint" (lines 49-51), it is not humility here that the author is praising, but Shakespeare's ability to lose himself in a role and present a convincing fiction, making (D) the correct choice.

○ #39—Refer back to the passage and consider each of the answer choices in light of the context. (A) and (C) cannot be substituted for "attest" given the phrasing of the sentence, while the degree implied by (B) does not fit.

(D) is the best choice, as it can be comfortably substituted for "attest" while retaining the meaning of the sentence.

- o #51—Consider both the information presented in the graphic and passage. Choice (A) is not supported by the graphs, while choices (C) and (D) are also not supported by the information presented. Only choice (B) makes sense in light of the associated graphic and the discussion in the passage of the detrimental effects of higher temperatures on crops.

Harder Grammar Errors (20 minutes)

1. Cover the material on pages 315-319 to explain parallel structure, misplaced modifiers, and logical comparison errors.

2. These grammar concepts may be new to many students, so make sure they see the difference between the correct and incorrect example sentences. You can supply additional examples for your students if necessary. Some further examples are provided below.

Additional Examples of Parallel Structure Errors:

- **Example 1:**

  - o *Incorrect:* While Taylor wanted to watch the football game and have attended the housewarming event, she only had time for one activity.
  - o *Correct:* While Taylor wanted to watch the football game and attend the housewarming event, she only had time for one activity.

- **Example 2:**

  - o *Incorrect:* The teacher suggested that the students complete some practice tests, review the relevant chapters, and to reread their notes in preparation for the exam.
  - o *Correct:* The teacher suggested that the students complete some practice tests, review the relevant chapters, and reread their notes in preparation for the exam.

ADDITIONAL EXAMPLES OF MISPLACED MODIFIER ERRORS:

- **Example 1:**

  - *Incorrect:* They carefully carried their group project to the science fair, delicate and fragile, and placed it on the table.
  - *Correct:* They carefully carried their group project, delicate and fragile, to the science fair and placed it on the table.

- **Example 2:**

  - *Incorrect:* While long and convoluted, Teresa crafted a well-researched argument in her paper that earned her the highest mark in the class.
  - *Correct:* While long and convoluted, the well-researched argument that Teresa crafted in her paper earned her the highest mark in the class.

ADDITIONAL EXAMPLES OF LOGICAL COMPARISON ERRORS:

- **Example 1:**

  - *Incorrect:* The attendees of the music festival were more boisterous than the food festival down the street.
  - *Correct:* The attendees of the music festival were more boisterous than those of the food festival down the street.

- **Example 2:**

  - *Incorrect:* The hawk's wings are much better adapted for flight than the penguin.
  - *Correct:* The hawk's wings are much better adapted for flight than the penguin's.

CONFUSED WORDS & IDIOMS (10 MINUTES)

1. Discuss the commonly confused words and idioms in the charts on pages 319-322. Make sure students understand the correct usage of the words by reviewing the example sentences, or asking students to create their own.

2. Encourage students to review these tables frequently until they have memorized the correct usage for each word. Understanding these words will also help them when they write the SAT Essay.

GRAMMAR ERROR PRACTICE (20 MINUTES)

1. Give students 15 minutes to complete the practice questions on page 323.

2. Discuss the answers using the answer key on page 324. Make sure to cover the type of grammar error being corrected in each sentence.

BREAK (10 MINUTES)

GRAPHICS (20 MINUTES)

1. Cover the material on pages 343-349 on Graphics. Make sure students understand totals and parts, as discussed on pages 345-346.

2. Give students 10 minutes to complete the practice questions on pages 349-350. Discuss the answers using the answer key on page 352.

ORGANIZING IDEAS (15 MINUTES)

1. Cover the material on pages 353-356 on Organizing Ideas. Make sure students understand how to use the common signal words in the chart on page 355.

2. Give students 5 minutes to complete the practice questions on pages 356-357. Discuss the answers using the answer key on page 358.

EFFECTIVE LANGUAGE USE (20 MINUTES)

1. Cover the material on pages 359–364 on Effective Language Use. Make sure students understand differences in style and tone as discussed on pages 362-364.

2. Give students 5 minutes to complete the practice questions on page 365. Discuss the answers using the answer key on page 366.

HOMEWORK

At the end of class, answer any questions and assign the homework:

Hours 15-16	
Assignment	Page(s)
Complete practice set on Expressing Ideas	367-374
Memorize roots 36-45 (to *spec*)	228-229

Hours 17-18

HEART OF ALGEBRA

Task	Materials *(All Pages in New SAT Guide)*	Time
Homework Review	Pgs. 367-374; 228-229	5 minutes
Vocabulary Quiz	Pgs. 227-239	10 minutes
Linear Functions	Pgs. 545-550	20 minutes
Interpreting Equations	Pgs. 551-556	25 minutes
Break		10 minutes
Graphing Equations	Pgs. 557-576	20 minutes
Practice Set	Pgs. 577-586	30 minutes

HOMEWORK REVIEW (5 MINUTES)

1. Use this time to review any questions or exercises that students had trouble with, or to quiz students on what strategies or information they read about in the New SAT Guide.

VOCABULARY QUIZ (10 MINUTES)

1. Spend 10 minutes quizzing your class on the roots, prefixes, and suffixes they previously learned for homework, along with words from the vocabulary list. You can call or write out roots or vocabulary words that students must identify either individually or in teams. You can also have students compose sentences using vocabulary words, or give examples of words that use certain roots, prefixes, and suffixes. See *Classroom Advice* for more ideas and information.

2. You can also give students a written quiz to complete. As an owner of this book you can download quizzes on roots, prefixes, suffixes, and vocabulary words for your use.

3. You can also complete the vocabulary quiz at another point during your class session, such as halfway through, to help break up other material and provide variety.

Linear Functions (20 minutes)

1. Cover the material on pages 545-547 on linear functions. Make sure students understand function notation as described on page 545.

2. Give students 12 minutes to complete the practice questions on pages 547-548. Discuss the answers using the answer key on page 550.

Interpreting Equations (25 minutes)

1. Cover the material on pages 551-554 on interpreting equations. Make sure students understand that they can translate words into variables and operations using the chart on page 552.

2. Give students 15 minutes to complete the practice questions on page 555. Discuss the answers using the answer key on page 556.

Break (10 minutes)

Graphing Equations (20 minutes)

1. Cover the material on pages 557-568 on graphing equations. Make sure students understand what different graphs look like by walking through the examples.

2. Give students 10 minutes to complete the practice questions on pages 569-572. Discuss the answers using the answer key on pages 574-576.

PRACTICE SET (30 MINUTES)

1. Give students time to complete the remaining questions in the Practice Set on pages 577-585. Discuss the answers using the answer key on pages 586.

2. You can have students attempt all questions before taking them up, or break part-way through to review the first half of the questions.

HOMEWORK

At the end of class, answer any questions and assign the homework:

Hours 17-18	
Assignment	Page(s)
Read and complete practice set on Polynomial Expressions	587-594
Memorize final 7 roots	229

HOURS 19-20

PASSPORT TO ADVANCED MATH + ANALYZING ARGUMENTS + PRACTICE ESSAY

Task	Materials (All Pages in New SAT Guide)	Time
Homework Review	Pgs. 587-594; 229	5 minutes
Factoring Polynomials	Pgs. 595-602	20 minutes
Language	Pgs. 401-405	10 minutes
Evidence	Pgs. 406-409	10 minutes
Organization & Reasoning	Pgs. 410-415	15 minutes
Break		10 minutes
Timed Practice Essay	Pgs. 440-441	50 minutes
Essay Marking	Pgs. 424-426	After class

HOMEWORK REVIEW (5 MINUTES)

1. Use this time to review any questions or exercises that students had trouble with, or to quiz students on what strategies or information they read about in the New SAT Guide.

FACTORING POLYNOMIALS (20 MINUTES)

1. Cover the material on pages 595-600 on factoring polynomials. Make sure students understand how to factor with quadratic trinomials and different values, as well as a difference of squares or cubes.

2. Give students 10 minutes to complete the practice questions on page 601. Discuss the answers using the answer key on page 602.

Language (10 minutes)

1. Cover the material on pages 401-404 on language use. Make sure students understand the concept of word connotation.

2. Give students 5 minutes to complete the first two practice questions on page 405. Discuss the answers as a class.

Evidence (10 minutes)

1. Cover the material on pages 406-408 on evidence. Make sure students can differentiate between the different types of evidence they may see.

2. Give students 5 minutes to complete the first two practice questions on page 409. Discuss the answers as a class.

Organization & Reasoning (15 minutes)

1. Cover the material on pages 410-414 on organization and reasoning. Make sure students understand how to track an argument throughout a passage using the "Deadbeat Dams" sample passage.

2. Give students 8 minutes to answer the practice questions on page 414. Discuss the answers as a class.

Break (10 minutes)

Timed Practice Essay (50 minutes)

1. Give students 50 minutes to write an essay using Essay Prompt #2 on pages 440-441. Students can write on a loose sheet of paper, which you will collect at the end.

2. Ensure there is a way for students to keep track of time. If there is no easily visible clock where you are teaching, you can run a countdown timer through a projection screen or mark the time remaining on a whiteboard or chalkboard.

3. Give your students a verbal 5-minute warning when they have 5 minutes left in the section. Say: "You now have 5 minutes left to complete this section."

ESSAY MARKING (AFTER CLASS)

1. Before the next class session mark each student's essay using the College Board's rubric provided on pages 424-426. Provide a score of 1-4 in each of Reading, Analysis, and Writing, with notes if applicable.

2. Provide comments on how to improve where appropriate, and indicate any relevant parts of the essay that demonstrate good work or could be edited. You may also note any issues with grammar, spelling, or diction.

HOMEWORK

At the end of class, answer any questions and assign the homework:

Hours 19-20	
Assignment	Page(s)
Review strategies for all sections, and all roots and vocabulary words in anticipation of diagnostic test	

HOURS 21-24
FULL-LENGTH DIAGNOSTIC TEST

Task	Materials	Time
Proctor Diagnostic Test	Diagnostic Test #1	4 hours
Prepare Score Report	Diagnostic Analysis Scoring Sheet	After class

PROCTOR DIAGNOSTIC TEST (4 HOURS)

1. Proctor a full-length diagnostic SAT for your class. Students must complete the sections in the order they are given, and can only work on one section at a time. The test sections always appear in the same order:

   - 65-minute Reading section
   - 25-minute No-calculator Math section
     - 5-minute Break
   - 35-minute Writing section
   - 55-minute Calculator Math section
     - 5-minute Break
   - 50-minute Essay

2. Provide a 5-minute break after the No-calculator Math section, and after the Calculator Math section if your students will be completing the Essay section.

3. Let the students know the order of test sections and breaks. Let students know that there is no penalty for wrong answers, so they are encouraged to guess on any questions they cannot complete. Students must mark down their answers on their bubble sheets, and not just in their test booklets.

4. Ensure there is a way for students to keep track of time. If there is no easily visible clock where you are teaching, you can run a countdown timer through a projection screen or mark the time remaining on a whiteboard or chalkboard.

5. Always give your students a verbal 5-minute warning when they have 5 minutes left in the section. Say: "You now have 5 minutes left to complete this section."

6. Maintain a realistic test-taking environment by not allowing talking, eating, outside notes, or the use of any electronic devices during the test. Students may use a calculator, including scientific or graphing calculator, during the Calculator Math section only.

7. Be sure students complete their test with an HB or #2 pencil. Pen marks will not show up on the SAT test and students could receive no credit for their answers or essay.

8. If this is your final class session, inform students that their scores will be sent to them within a few days. You can email student scores and/or make them available for pick-up by students and parents. See *Classroom Advice* for more information on diagnostics.

9. If this is not your final class session, aim to have Score Reports prepared to return to your students at the next class session if possible.

Download printable answer sheets (PDF) at:
ivyglobal.com/teach

PREPARE SCORE REPORT (AFTER CLASS)

1. Follow the instructions on the Diagnostic Analysis Scoring Sheet to prepare a Score Report for each student. You will complete this after the class.

2. Send out Score Reports for students or make them available for pick-up if your course is complete. Return Score Reports during your next class session if your class will continue.

Section 4
36-Hour Course Curriculum

The 36-hour course consists of the following curriculum pages built on top of the previous 12-hour and 24-hour courses. To complete the full 36-hour course first work through hours 1-12 from the 12-hour course, hours 13-24 from the 24-hour course, and then continue with the following pages to work through hours 25-36.

HOURS 25-26

Task	Materials (All Pages in New SAT Guide)	Time
Homework Review		5 minutes
Vocabulary Quiz	Pgs. 227-239	10 minutes
Words & Phrases in Context	Pgs. 108-114	10 minutes
Explicit & Implicit Meaning	Pgs. 115-122	15 minutes
Central Ideas & Relationships	Pgs. 123-130	20 minutes
Break		10 minutes
Evidence in a Passage	Pgs. 131-136	15 minutes
Analogical Reasoning	Pgs. 137-142	15 minutes
Understanding the Facts Practice Set	Pgs. 143-146; 150	20 minutes

HOMEWORK REVIEW (5 MINUTES)

1. Use this time to review any questions or exercises that students had trouble with, or to quiz students on what strategies or information they read about in the New SAT Guide.

VOCABULARY QUIZ (10 MINUTES)

1. Spend 10 minutes quizzing your class on the roots, prefixes, and suffixes they previously learned for homework, along with words from the vocabulary list. You can call or write out roots or vocabulary words that students must identify either individually or in teams. You can also have students compose sentences using vocabulary words, or give examples of words that use certain roots, prefixes, and suffixes. See *Classroom Advice* for more ideas and information.

2. You can also give students a written quiz to complete. As an owner of this book you can download quizzes on roots, prefixes, suffixes, and vocabulary words for your use.

3. You can also complete the vocabulary quiz at another point during your class session, such as halfway through, to help break up other material and provide variety.

WORDS & PHRASES IN CONTEXT (10 MINUTES)

1. Cover the material on pages 108-111 on Information and Ideas questions, and the first type, Words and Phrases in Context questions. Make sure students understand that they are looking for a synonym of the word in question, and strategies for reaching the answer.

2. Give students 3 minutes to complete the practice questions on page 111-112. Discuss the answers using the answer key on page 114.

EXPLICIT & IMPLICIT MEANING (15 MINUTES)

1. Cover the material on pages 115-118 on explicit and implicit meaning questions. Make sure students understand the difference between the two question types, and the question wording that indicates an implicit meaning question, as discussed on page 117.

2. Give students 8 minutes to read the passage and complete the practice questions on pages 119-120. Discuss how students marked up their passage as a class, and then discuss the answers using the answer key on page 122.

Central Ideas & Relationships (20 minutes)

1. Cover the material on pages 123-127 on central ideas and relationships questions. Make sure students understand the difference between the two question types, and the importance of referring back to the passage to answer them both.

2. Give students 5 minutes to read the passage and complete the practice questions on page 127-128. Discuss how students marked up their passage as a class, and then discuss the answers using the answer key on page 130.

Break (10 minutes)

Evidence in a Passage (15 minutes)

1. Cover the material on pages 131-134 on evidence questions. Make sure students understand how these questions will be paired with another, previous question as discussed on page 131.

2. Give students 8 minutes to read the passage and complete the practice questions on pages 134-135. Discuss the answers using the answer key on page 136.

Analogical Reasoning (15 minutes)

1. Cover the material on pages 137-138 on analogical reasoning. Make sure students understand what an analogy is, as discussed in page 137.

2. Give students 5 minutes to complete the practice questions on pages 139-140. Discuss the answers using the answer key on page 142.

UNDERSTANDING THE FACTS PRACTICE SET (20 MINUTES)

1. Give students 5 minutes to read the practice passage on page 143-144. Pause to discuss how students marked up the passage, and the summaries they made for each paragraph.

2. Then give students 8 minutes to answer the questions about the passage on pages 144-146. Discuss the answers using the answer key on page 150.

HOMEWORK

At the end of class, answer any questions and assign the homework:

Hours 25-26	
Assignment	Page(s)
Complete Understanding the Facts Practice Set	146-150
Complete the practice passage, aiming to complete it in under 15 minutes	249-250

Hours 27-28
Writing Test Review & Practice

Task	Materials *(All Pages in New SAT Guide)*	Time
Homework Review	Pgs. 146-150; 249-250	5 minutes
Vocabulary Quiz	Pgs. 227-239	10 minutes
Review Grammar Basics	Pgs. 284-302	15 minutes
Review Common Grammar Errors	Pgs. 303-314	20 minutes
Review Harder Grammar Errors	Pgs. 315-324; Confused Words & Idioms Quiz	20 minutes
Break		10 minutes
Grammar Practice Set	Pgs. 325-334	40 minutes

Homework Review (5 minutes)

1. Use this time to review any questions or exercises that students had trouble with, or to quiz students on what strategies or information they read about in the New SAT Guide.

Vocabulary Quiz (10 minutes)

1. Spend 10 minutes quizzing your class on the roots, prefixes, and suffixes they previously learned for homework, along with words from the vocabulary list. You can call or write out roots or vocabulary words that students must identify either individually or in teams. You can also have students compose sentences using vocabulary words, or give examples of words that use certain roots, prefixes, and suffixes. See *Classroom Advice* for more ideas and information.

2. You can also give students a written quiz to complete. As an owner of this book you can download quizzes on roots, prefixes, suffixes, and vocabulary words for your use.

Download handouts (PDF) at:

ivyglobal.com/teach

3. You can also complete the vocabulary quiz at another point during your class session, such as halfway through, to help break up other material and provide variety.

REVIEW GRAMMAR BASICS (15 MINUTES)

1. Because grammar concepts are new to many students, it is important to review them. Ask students about parts of speech, such as nouns and pronouns, verbs, adjectives and adverbs, using pages 284-288 for reference.

2. You can ask students to give examples of each category, and then write sentences on a board or say them aloud and have students identify the different parts. Use the example sentences in the New SAT for inspiration to compose your own similar examples.

3. Next ask students about sentences, including subjects and objects, verb tenses, and independent and dependent clauses, using pages 289-302 for reference.

4. You can write sentences on a board or read them aloud and ask students if they should use the subject or object case, or what verb tense is required. You can also ask students to compose their own sentences that properly use subordinating conjunctions, coordinating conjunctions, or conjunction pairs. You can write dependent clauses on the board or say them aloud, and ask students how they could rewrite each clause to make it independent instead. You can also quiz students on the proper use of semicolons, colons, and commas.

REVIEW COMMON GRAMMAR ERRORS (20 MINUTES)

1. Students should also be familiar with the types of errors they are most likely to see. Quiz students on common grammar errors involving complete sentences, verb and pronoun shifts, and tense, voice, and mood shifts, using pages 303-314.

2. You can write sentences on a board or read them aloud and ask students whether they are complete sentences or fragments. If they are fragments, ask students how they could correct them.

3. You can write sentences on a board or read them aloud and ask students to pick which verb or pronoun they should use. You can also quiz students on singular pronouns using the chart on page 308.

4. You can write sentences on a board or read them aloud and ask students to correct shifts in verb tense, passive and active voice, and mood.

REVIEW HARDER GRAMMAR ERRORS (20 MINUTES)

1. Next, review harder grammar errors with students. Quiz students on parallel structure, misplaced modifiers, logical comparison errors, and confused words and idioms using pages 315-324.

2. You can write sentences on a board or read them aloud and ask students to alter them so that they follow a parallel structure. You can also ask students to give their own examples of parallel sentences.

3. You can write sentences with misplaced modifiers on a board or read them aloud and ask students to correct them so that it is clear what each clause is modifying.

4. You can write sentences on a board or read them aloud and ask students to correct errors in logical comparison.

5. You can quiz students on words and idioms using the tables on pages 320-322. You can also give students the written Confused Words & Idioms quiz, which you can modify or adapt to suit the needs of your class. Give students 8 minutes to complete the quiz. Discuss the answers as a class using the Teacher Answer Key.

Download handouts (PDF) at:
ivyglobal.com/teach

BREAK (10 MINUTES)

GRAMMAR PRACTICE SET (40 MINUTES)

1. Look over the Section Review on pages 325-326. Encourage students to return to this resource to refresh their knowledge and see which pages to review for concepts they are struggling with.

2. Next, give students 12 minutes to complete the first 15 questions in the practice set on pgs. 327-332. For each question, have students select their answer and also identify the category of error. For example, question #1 has an error with subjects and objects; the object "me" is used instead of the subject "I." Discuss the answers and the category of error using the answer key on page 334.

3. Give students another 12 minutes complete the remaining questions, again identifying the category of error for each one. Discuss the answers and the category of error using the answer key on page 334.

HOMEWORK

At the end of class, answer any questions and assign the homework:

Hours 27-28	
Assignment	Page(s)
Complete full practice set in 35 minutes or less	375-382
Memorize prefixes 1-10 (to *extro*) on the Prefixes list; Memorize Vocabulary words 61-80	229; 233

Hours 29-30

Advanced Math Continued

Task	Materials *(All Pages in New SAT Guide)*	Time
Homework Review	Pgs. 375-382;	5 minutes
Quadratic Functions	Pgs. 611-620	25 minutes
Advanced Equations	Pgs. 621-628	20 minutes
Break		10 minutes
Applications of Functions	Pgs. 629-636	25 minutes
Passport to Advanced Math Practice Set	Pgs. 637-643; 646	35 minutes

Homework Review (5 minutes)

1. Use this time to review any questions or exercises that students had trouble with, or to quiz students on what strategies or information they read about in the New SAT Guide.

Quadratic Functions (25 minutes)

1. Cover the material on pages 611-617 on quadratic functions. Make sure students understand how to graph a parabola as explained on page 612, as well as how to make transformations of quadratic functions as demonstrated on pages 613-615.

2. Give students 12 minutes to complete the practice questions on pages 618-619. Discuss the answers using the answer key on page 620.

ADVANCED EQUATIONS (20 MINUTES)

1. Cover the material on pages 621-625 on advanced equations. Make sure students understand exponential, rational, and radical equations.

2. Give students 12 minutes to complete the practice questions on pages 625-626. Discuss the answers using the answer key on page 628.

BREAK (10 MINUTES)

APPLICATIONS OF FUNCTIONS (25 MINUTES)

1. Cover the material on pages 629-633 on applications of functions. Make sure students understand the real-world applications of functions, as well as how to compare equations as explained by the chart on page 632.

2. Give students 15 minutes to complete the practice questions on pages 633-634. Discuss the answers using the answer key on page 636. Explanations for some of the more challenging questions are given below.

   o #1. When the basin is empty, the volume of water in the basin is 0. So we set $V = 0$ in our equation and solve for time t.

   - $0 = t^2 - 24t + 144$ Factor and solve for x
   - $0 = (t - 12)^2$ So **$t = 12$ seconds**

   o #4. Paul threw the book at time $= 0$, so to determine how far Paul was holding the book when he threw it, we are essentially finding the height h at $t = 0$. Plugging in $t = 0$, we get:

   - $h = -(0)^2 + 3(0) + 4$
   - **$h = 4$ meters**

Passport to Advanced Math Practice Set (35 minutes)

1. Give students 25 minutes to complete practice questions #1-20 on pages 637-643.

2. Discuss the answers using the answer key on page 646. You can review any topics from that students had trouble with by referring back to the relevant part in the Section, which begins on page 587. Explanations for some of the more challenging questions are given below.

   ○ #5. Since $f(3) = 3^2 + 1 = 9 + 1 = 10$, we have

   $$f(f(3)) = f(10) = 10^2 + 1 = 100 + 1 = \mathbf{101}$$

   ○ #15. Since the leading coefficient is negative, we know that the vertex is at a maximum (so right away we can eliminate answer choices (A) and (C)). Now we can complete the square to determine which quadrant the vertex is at.

   $$y = -x^2 - 2bx - b^2 + c = -(x^2 + 2bx + b^2 - b^2) - b^2 + c$$
   $$= -(x + b)^2 + b^2 - b^2 + c = -(x + b)^2 + c$$

   So the coordinates of the vertex are $(-b, c)$. Since $b > 0$ and $c > 0$, the vertex lies in the second quadrant. Since the graph in answer choice (D) lies in the second quadrant *and* is a downward facing parabola, the correct **answer choice is (D)**.

Homework

At the end of class, answer any questions and assign the homework:

Hours 29-30	
Assignment	Page(s)
Complete questions #21-30 in the Passport to Advanced Math Practice Set	643-646
Memorize Prefixes 11-20 (to *post*); Memorize Vocabulary words 81-100	229-230; 233-234

Hours 31-32

Problem Solving + Essay Practice

Task	Materials *(All Pages in New SAT Guide)*	Time
Homework Review		5 minutes
Measurement and Units	Pgs. 647-656	25 minutes
Essay Structure Review	Pgs. 395-398	5 minutes
Essay Prompt Analysis	Pgs. 440-441	10 minutes
Introduction		10 minutes
Break		10 minutes
Body Paragraph 1		15 minutes
Body Paragraphs 2-4		20 minutes
Conclusion		10 minutes
Peer Revision	Pgs. 424-426	10 minutes

HOMEWORK REVIEW (5 MINUTES)

1. Use this time to review any questions or exercises that students had trouble with, or to quiz students on what strategies or information they read about in the New SAT Guide.

MEASUREMENT AND UNITS (25 MINUTES)

1. Cover the material on pages 647-653 on measurement and units. Make sure students understand converting between units as explained on pages 649-650, and using units in word problems.

2. Give students 10 minutes to complete the practice questions on pages 653-654. Discuss the answers using the answer key on page 656.

Essay Structure Review (5 minutes)

1. Review the material on pages 395-398 on structuring an essay. Make sure students understand what to include in an introduction, body paragraph, and conclusion.

2. Before having students refer to the information in their New SAT Guides, you can call on them to describe what should be included in each portion of the essay, or invite students to write down key points on the board.

Essay Prompt Analysis (10 minutes)

1. Give students 5 minutes to read and analyze Essay Prompt #2 on pages 440-441. Make sure they consider or mark up how the author uses language, evidence, and organization and reasoning to make his argument.

2. Next, lead a short discussion with students about how these how each of these elements is used in the prompt passage, and/or make notes about them on the board as they are mentioned.

3. Next, ask students if they can see themes emerging that they can use to tie these elements together to write a cohesive essay.

Introduction (10 minutes)

1. Give students 5 minutes to brainstorm further, and write an essay introduction in response to the prompt.

2. Discuss the introductions as a class, asking for students to read out their introductions or certain sentences. Make sure that students have included a clear thesis which briefly mentions their supporting arguments.

Break (10 minutes)

Body Paragraph 1 (15 minutes)

1. Give students 10 minutes to write their essay's first body paragraph.

2. Discuss the body paragraphs as a class, asking for students to describe the point of their paragraph, or to read out certain sentences. Make sure that students have included a topic sentence, 3-4 supporting sentences, and a concluding sentence.

3. You can also ask students what transitions they have used between their sentences.

Body Paragraphs 2-4 (20 minutes)

1. Give students 15 minutes to write their next 2-3 body paragraphs.

2. Discuss the body paragraphs as a class, asking for students to describe the point of their paragraph, or to read out certain sentences. Make sure that students have included a topic sentence, 3-4 supporting sentences, and a concluding sentence.

3. You can also ask students what transitions they have used between their sentences.

Conclusion (10 minutes)

1. Give students 5 minutes to write their conclusions.

2. Discuss the conclusions as a class, asking for students to read out their conclusions, or certain sentences. Make sure that students have included a topic sentence, 3-4 supporting sentences, and a concluding sentence.

3. You can also ask students to double-check that they have not added in any new information in their conclusion.

Peer Revision (10 minutes)

1. Have students swap essays with their peers. To make it easy have each student pass their essay to the person on their right, so everyone ends up with a different essay.

2. Have students read over the essays, while referring to the College Board rubric on pages 424-426, to recall what the essays should contain. Ask students to try to identify 1 or 2 things they think could be improved upon on the essay, and 1 or 2 things that are done well in the essay. Students are not to provide a grade to the essay, but rather to leave general comments.

Homework

At the end of class, answer any questions and assign the homework:

Hours 31-32	
Assignment	Page(s)
Read and complete practice questions on Properties of Data	657-672
Students should review the comments on their essay	
Review all strategies and content from this part of the course for diagnostic next class	

Hours 33-36

Diagnostic Test

Task	Materials (All Pages in New SAT Guide)	Time
Proctor Diagnostic Test	Diagnostic Test #2	4 hours
Prepare Score Report	Diagnostic Analysis Scoring Sheet	After class

Proctor Diagnostic Test (4 hours)

1. Proctor a full-length diagnostic SAT for your class. Students must complete the sections in the order they are given, and can only work on one section at a time. The test sections always appear in the same order:

    - 65-minute Reading section
    - 25-minute No-calculator Math section
      - 5-minute Break
    - 35-minute Writing section
    - 55-minute Calculator Math section
      - 5-minute Break
    - 50-minute Essay

2. Provide a 5-minute break after the No-calculator Math section, and after the Calculator Math section if your students will be completing the Essay section.

3. Let the students know the order of test sections and breaks. Let students know that there is no penalty for wrong answers, so they are encouraged to guess on any questions they cannot complete. Students must mark down their answers on their bubble sheets, and not just in their test booklets.

4. Ensure there is a way for students to keep track of time. If there is no easily visible clock where you are teaching, you can run a countdown timer through a projection screen or mark the time remaining on a whiteboard or chalkboard.

5. Always give your students a verbal 5-minute warning when they have 5 minutes left in the section. Say: "You now have 5 minutes left to complete this section."

6. Maintain a realistic test-taking environment by not allowing talking, eating, outside notes, or the use of any electronic devices during the test. Students may use a calculator, including scientific or graphing calculator, during the Calculator Math section only.

7. Be sure students complete their test with an HB or #2 pencil. Pen marks will not show up on the SAT test and students could receive no credit for their answers or essay.

8. If this is your final class session, inform students that their scores will be sent to them within a few days. You can email student scores and/or make them available for pick-up by students and parents. See *Classroom Advice* for more information on diagnostics.

9. If this is not your final class session, aim to have Score Reports prepared to return to your students at the next class session if possible.

Download printable answer sheets (PDF) at:
ivyglobal.com/teach

PREPARE SCORE REPORT (AFTER CLASS)

1. Follow the instructions on the Diagnostic Analysis Scoring Sheet to prepare a Score Report for each student. You will complete this after the class.

2. Send out Score Reports for students or make them available for pick-up if your course is complete. Return Score Reports during your next class session if your class will continue.

48-HOUR COURSE CURRICULUM

The 48-hour course consists of the following curriculum pages built on top of the previous 12-hour, 24-hour courses and 36-hour courses. To complete the full 48-hour course first work through hours 1-36 from those courses, and then continue with the following pages to work through hours 37-48.

HOURS 37-38

Task	Materials (All Pages in New SAT Guide)	Time
Homework Review		5 minutes
Analyzing Word Choice	Pgs. 152-158	15 minutes
Analyzing Text Structure	Pgs. 159-164	10 minutes
Point of View & Purpose	Pgs. 165-170	10 minutes
Analyzing Arguments	Pgs. 171-180	20 minutes
Break		10 minutes
Writing Review	Pgs. 263-280	5 minutes
Writing Practice	Pgs. 375-382	45 minutes

HOMEWORK REVIEW (5 MINUTES)

1. Use this time to review any questions or exercises that students had trouble with, or to quiz students on what strategies or information they read about in the New SAT Guide.

ANALYZING WORD CHOICE (15 MINUTES)

1. Cover the material on pages 152-156 on the Persuasive Language category of questions, and Analyzing Word Choice questions. Make sure students recall rhetorical devices, and understand the tone words on page 155.

2. Give students 5 minutes to complete the practice questions on pages 156-157. Discuss the answers using the answer key on page 158.

ANALYZING TEXT STRUCTURE (10 MINUTES)

1. Cover the material on pages 159-162 on analyzing text structure questions. Make sure students understand how to mark up the structure of a passage, as shown on page 162.

2. Give students 5 minutes to read and mark up the practice passage, and complete the questions on pages 162-163. Discuss the answers using the answer key on page 164.

POINT OF VIEW & PURPOSE (10 MINUTES)

1. Cover the material on pages 165-167 on point of view and purpose questions. Make sure students understand the difference between the two question types.

2. Give students 5 minutes to complete the practice questions on page 168. Discuss the answers using the answer key on page 170.

ANALYZING ARGUMENTS (20 MINUTES)

1. Cover the material on pages 171-176 on analyzing arguments questions. Make sure students understand the definition of a counterclaim, and different types of evidence, as explained in the chart on page 173.

2. Give students 8 minutes to read and mark up the practice passage and complete the questions on page 176-178. Discuss the answers using the answer key on page 180.

BREAK (10 MINUTES)

WRITING REVIEW (5 MINUTES)

1. Review the material on approaching the Writing section, using pages 263-280 for reference. Make sure students remember how to read the entire passage and work

on one passage at a time; that they can read passages and attempt questions out of order; and how to use the process of elimination and guessing.

WRITING PRACTICE (45 MINUTES)

1. Give students 35 minutes to complete the full Writing section on pages 375-382.

2. Ensure there is a way for students to keep track of time. If there is no easily visible clock where you are teaching, you can run a countdown timer through a projection screen or mark the time remaining on a whiteboard or chalkboard.

3. Give your students a verbal 5-minute warning when they have 5 minutes left in the section. Say: "You now have 5 minutes left to complete this section."

4. Maintain a realistic test-taking environment by not allowing talking, eating, outside notes, or the use of any electronic devices during the section.

5. Discuss the answers using the answer key on page 384 and the full answer explanations.

View full answer explanations at:
ivyglobal.com/teach

HOMEWORK

At the end of class, answer any questions and assign the homework:

Hours 37-38	
Assignment	Page(s)
Complete the Persuasive Language practice set, aiming to complete in 20 minutes or less	181-188
Memorize the final 7 prefixes; Memorize Vocabulary words 101-120	230; 234-235

Hours 39-40
Reading: Combining Ideas + Math Practice

Task	Materials (All Pages in New SAT Guide)	Time
Homework Review	Pgs. 181-188; 230; 234-235	5 minutes
Vocabulary quiz	Pgs. 227-239	15 minutes
Paired Passages	Pgs. 190-198; 101-102	20 minutes
Passages with Graphs	Pgs. 199-206; 95-96	20 minutes
Break		10 minutes
Passage Practice	Pgs. 207-210; 216	15 minutes
Math Practice Set	Pgs. 822-828	35 minutes

Homework Review (5 minutes)

1. Use this time to review any questions or exercises that students had trouble with, or to quiz students on what strategies or information they read about in the New SAT Guide.

Vocabulary Quiz (15 minutes)

1. Spend 15 minutes quizzing your class on the roots, prefixes, and suffixes they previously learned for homework, along with words from the vocabulary list. You can call or write out roots or vocabulary words that students must identify either individually or in teams. You can also have students compose sentences using vocabulary words, or give examples of words that use certain roots, prefixes, and suffixes. See *Classroom Advice* for more ideas and information.

2. You can also give students a written quiz to complete. As an owner of this book you can download quizzes on roots, prefixes, suffixes, and vocabulary words for your use.

3. You can also complete the vocabulary quiz at another point during your class session, such as halfway through, to help break up other material and provide variety.

PAIRED PASSAGES (20 MINUTES)

1. Cover the material on pages 190-194 on paired passages. Make sure students understand how to find repeated ideas across passages and practice with the sample passage on pages 193-194. You can also review the information on paired passages previously covered on pages 101-102.

2. Give students 3 minutes to read and mark up the practice passages on pages 194-195. Discuss them as a class. Then give students 5 minutes to answer the questions on pages 196-197. Discuss the answers using the answer key on page 198.

PASSAGES WITH GRAPHS (20 MINUTES)

1. Cover the material on pages 199-202 on passages with graphs. Make sure students understand how to read the sample graphics, and how to relate graphics to passages as discussed on pages 200-202. You can also review the information on graphics previously covered on pages 95-96.

2. Give students 5 minutes to complete the practice questions on page 203. Discuss the answers using the answer key on page 206. Then give students 5 minutes to complete the practice questions on pages 204-205, again discussing the answers using the answer key on page 206.

BREAK (10 MINUTES)

Passage Practice (15 minutes)

1. Give students 5 minutes to read and mark up the paired passages on pages 207-208. Discuss the main ideas in each passage, and the relationship between them.

2. Then give students 5 minutes to answer the questions on pages 208-210. Discuss the answers using the answer key on page 216.

Math Practice (35 minutes)

1. Give students 25 minutes to complete the full Math no-calculator section on pages 822-827.

2. Ensure there is a way for students to keep track of time. If there is no easily visible clock where you are teaching, you can run a countdown timer through a projection screen or mark the time remaining on a whiteboard or chalkboard.

3. Give your students a verbal 5-minute warning when they have 5 minutes left in the section. Say: "You now have 5 minutes left to complete this section."

4. Maintain a realistic test-taking environment by not allowing talking, eating, outside notes, or the use of any electronic devices during the section. Because this is a no-calculator section, no calculators may be used.

5. Discuss the answers using the answer key on page 828 and the full answer explanations.

View full answer explanations at:
ivyglobal.com/teach

Homework

At the end of class, answer any questions and assign the homework:

Hours 39-40	
Assignment	Page(s)
Finish the Combining Ideas Practice passages	211-216
Memorize the first 10 suffixes from the Suffix list (to *–ful*); Memorize Vocabulary words 121-140	230; 235

HOURS 41-42
MATH: PROBLEM SOLVING & DATA ANALYSIS CONTINUED

Task	Materials (All Pages in New SAT Guide)	Time
Homework Review	211-216; 230; 235	5 minutes
Vocabulary quiz	Pgs. 227-239	10 minutes
Ratios, Percentages, Proportions, and Rates	Pgs. 673-680	20 minutes
Probability and Statistics	Pgs. 681-700	40 minutes
Break		10 minutes
Modeling Data	Pgs. 701-710	20 minutes
Using Data as Evidence	Pgs. 711-718	15 minutes

HOMEWORK REVIEW (5 MINUTES)

1. Use this time to review any questions or exercises that students had trouble with, or to quiz students on what strategies or information they read about in the New SAT Guide.

VOCABULARY QUIZ (10 MINUTES)

1. Spend 15 minutes quizzing your class on the roots, prefixes, and suffixes they previously learned for homework, along with words from the vocabulary list. You can call or write out roots or vocabulary words that students must identify either individually or in teams. You can also have students compose sentences using vocabulary words, or give examples of words that use certain roots, prefixes, and suffixes. See *Classroom Advice* for more ideas and information.

2. You can also give students a written quiz to complete. As an owner of this book you can download quizzes on roots, prefixes, suffixes, and vocabulary words for your use.

3. You can also complete the vocabulary quiz at another point during your class session, such as halfway through, to help break up other material and provide variety.

RATIOS, PERCENTAGES, PROPORTIONS, AND RATES (20 MINUTES)

1. Cover the material on pages 673-678 on ratios, percentages, proportions, and rates. Make sure students understand the differences between the four concepts.

2. Give students 12 minutes to complete the practice questions on page 679. Discuss the answers using the answer key on page 680.

PROBABILITY AND STATISTICS (40 MINUTES)

1. Cover the material on pages 681-697 on probability and statistics. Make sure students understand how to use the counting principle as described on pages 683-684, and conditional probability, explained on pages 692-694.

2. Give students 15 minutes to complete the practice questions on pages 698-699. Discuss the answers using the answer key on page 700.

BREAK (10 MINUTES)

MODELING DATA (20 MINUTES)

1. Cover the material on pages 701-704 on modeling data. Make sure students understand how to estimate using a trend line, as described on pages 702-704.

2. Give students 10 minutes to complete the practice questions on pages 705-708. Discuss the answers using the answer key on page 710.

USING DATA AS EVIDENCE (15 MINUTES)

1. Cover the material on pages 711-718 on using data as evidence. Make sure students understand how to interpret data, as well as margins of error as explained on pages 717-718.

2. Students will complete the practice set in this section for homework.

HOMEWORK

At the end of class, answer any questions and assign the homework:

Hours 40-41	
Assignment	Page(s)
Complete Using Data as Evidence practice set	718-722
Complete Problem Solving & Data Analysis practice set	723-734

HOURS 43-44
MATH PRACTICE + ESSAY PRACTICE

Task	Materials (All Pages in New SAT Guide)	Time
Homework Review	Pgs. 718-734	5 minutes
Math Practice	Pgs. 809-818	1 hour
Break		5 minutes
Essay Practice	Pgs. 442-443	50 minutes
Essay Marking	Pgs. 424-426	After class

HOMEWORK REVIEW (5 MINUTES)

1. Use this time to review any questions or exercises that students had trouble with, or to quiz students on what strategies or information they read about in the New SAT Guide.

MATH PRACTICE (1 HOUR)

1. Give students 55 minutes to complete the full Math Calculator section on pages 809-818.

2. Ensure there is a way for students to keep track of time. If there is no easily visible clock where you are teaching, you can run a countdown timer through a projection screen or mark the time remaining on a whiteboard or chalkboard.

3. Give your students a verbal 5-minute warning when they have 5 minutes left in the section. Say: "You now have 5 minutes left to complete this section."

4. Maintain a realistic test-taking environment by not allowing talking, eating, outside notes, or the use of any electronic devices during the test. Students may use a calculator.

5. Discuss the answers using the answer key on pages 820-821 and the full answer explanations.

> View full answer explanations at:
> ivyglobal.com/teach

BREAK (5 MINUTES)

ESSAY PRACTICE (50 MINUTES)

1. Give students 50 minutes to write an essay using Essay Prompt #3 on pages 442-443. Students can write on a loose sheet of paper, which you will collect at the end.

2. Ensure there is a way for students to keep track of time. If there is no easily visible clock where you are teaching, you can run a countdown timer through a projection screen or mark the time remaining on a whiteboard or chalkboard.

3. Give your students a verbal 5-minute warning when they have 5 minutes left to finish their essays. Say: "You now have 5 minutes left to complete this section."

ESSAY MARKING (AFTER CLASS)

1. Before the next class session mark each student's essay using the College Board's rubric provided on pages 424-426. Provide a score of 1-4 in each of Reading, Analysis, and Writing, with notes if applicable.

2. Provide comments on how to improve where appropriate, and indicate any relevant parts of the essay that demonstrate good work or could be edited. You may also note any issues with grammar, spelling, or diction.

HOMEWORK

At the end of class, answer any questions and assign the homework:

Hours 42-43	
Assignment	Page(s)
Review all strategies and content from this part of the course for diagnostic next class	

Hours 45-48

Diagnostic Test

Task	Materials	Time
Proctor Diagnostic Test	New SAT Guide Practice Test #1 pgs. 833-877	4 hours
Prepare Score Report	Diagnostic Analysis Scoring Sheet	After class

Proctor Diagnostic Test (4 hours)

1. Proctor a full-length diagnostic SAT for your class. Students must complete the sections in the order they are given, and can only work on one section at a time. The test sections always appear in the same order:

    -   65-minute Reading section
    -   25-minute No-calculator Math section
        -   5-minute Break
    -   35-minute Writing section
    -   55-minute Calculator Math section
        -   5-minute Break
    -   50-minute Essay

2. Provide a 5-minute break after the No-calculator Math section, and after the Calculator Math section if your students will be completing the Essay section.

3. Let the students know the order of test sections and breaks. Let students know that there is no penalty for wrong answers, so they are encouraged to guess on any questions they cannot complete. Students must mark down their answers on their bubble sheets, and not just in their test booklets.

4. Ensure there is a way for students to keep track of time. If there is no easily visible clock where you are teaching, you can run a countdown timer through a projection screen or mark the time remaining on a whiteboard or chalkboard.

5. Always give your students a verbal 5-minute warning when they have 5 minutes left in the section. Say: "You now have 5 minutes left to complete this section."

6. Maintain a realistic test-taking environment by not allowing talking, eating, outside notes, or the use of any electronic devices during the test. Students may use a calculator, including scientific or graphing calculator, during the Calculator Math section only.

7. Be sure students complete their test with an HB or #2 pencil. Pen marks will not show up on the SAT test and students could receive no credit for their answers or essay.

8. If this is your final class session, inform students that their scores will be sent to them within a few days. You can email student scores and/or make them available for pick-up by students and parents. See *Classroom Advice* for more information on diagnostics.

9. If this is not your final class session, aim to have Score Reports prepared to return to your students at the next class session if possible.

Download printable answer sheets (PDF) at:

ivyglobal.com/teach

PREPARE SCORE REPORT (AFTER CLASS)

1. Follow the instructions on the Diagnostic Analysis Scoring Sheet to prepare a Score Report for each student. You will complete this after the class.

2. Send out Score Reports for students or make them available for pick-up if your course is complete. Return Score Reports during your next class session if your class will continue.

Section 6
60-Hour Course Curriculum

The 60-hour course consists of the following curriculum pages built on top of the previous 12-hour, 24-hour, 36-hour and 48-hour courses. To complete the full 60-hour course first work through hours 1-48 from those courses, and then continue with the following pages to work through hours 49-60.

Hours 49-50

Reading + Writing Review and Practice

Task	Materials (All Pages in New SAT Guide)	Time
Homework Review		5 minutes
Vocabulary quiz	Pgs. 227-239	10 minutes
Reading Review	Pgs. 34-58	15 minutes
Reading Practice Passage	Pgs. 251-252	20 minutes
Writing Grammar Review	Pgs. 283-324; Common Grammar Errors Worksheet	15 minutes
Break		10 minutes
Writing Practice Set	Pgs. 913-920; 934	45 minutes

Homework Review (5 minutes)

1. Use this time to review any questions or exercises that students had trouble with, or to quiz students on what strategies or information they read about in the New SAT Guide.

Vocabulary Quiz (10 minutes)

1. Spend 10 minutes quizzing your class on the roots, prefixes, and suffixes they previously learned for homework, along with words from the vocabulary list. You can call or write out roots or vocabulary words that students must identify either individually or in teams. You can also have students compose sentences using vocabulary words, or give examples of words that use certain roots, prefixes, and suffixes. See *Classroom Advice* for more ideas and information.

2. You can also give students a written quiz to complete. As an owner of this book you can download quizzes on roots, prefixes, suffixes, and vocabulary words for your use.

3. You can also complete the vocabulary quiz at another point during your class session, such as halfway through, to help break up other material and provide variety.

READING REVIEW (15 MINUTES)

1. Review the strategies and approach to the reading section using pages 34-58 for reference. Make sure students remember that they can approach the passages and questions out of order, and know how to mark up and summarize a passage.

2. You can quiz your class on the approach to the Reading Test by calling on different students to name the different steps they should take, and in what order. You can also ask students to go into detail on what they should mark up in a passage, building off of the 5 W's as discussed on pages 36-37.

3. Also be sure to review the importance of referring back to the passage to answer questions, as discussed on pages 47-49, as well as how to guess.

READING PRACTICE PASSAGE (20 MINUTES)

1. Give students 5 minutes to read, mark up, and make summaries for the passage on page 251. Then discuss the passage as a class, making sure students understand the main ideas in the passage.

2. Next give students 8 minutes to answer the questions on page 252. Discuss the answers using the answer key on page 254.

Writing Grammar Review (15 minutes)

1. Review all SAT grammar that has been covered during the course using pages 283-324 for reference. Depending on the needs and performance of your class you may choose to review the more basic concepts, such as parts of speech, or focus on the most challenging types of grammar errors, such as misplaced modifiers.

2. You can quiz students by having them correct sentences that you write on the board or say aloud, or by having them compose their own grammatically correct sentences. You can also ask students to define the role of different parts of speech or explain different grammar rules or constructions.

3. You can also have students work in teams to quiz each other, or to compose sentences with errors that the other team must correct.

4. You can also have students complete the Common Grammar Errors Worksheet, which you can download as an owner of this guide.

> Download handouts (PDF) at:
> ivyglobal.com/teach

Break (10 minutes)

Writing Practice Set (45 minutes)

1. Give students 35 minutes to complete the full Writing Section from the second full Practice Test on pages 913-920.

2. Ensure there is a way for students to keep track of time. If there is no easily visible clock where you are teaching, you can run a countdown timer through a projection screen or mark the time remaining on a whiteboard or chalkboard.

3. Give your students a verbal 5-minute warning when they have 5 minutes left in the section. Say: "You now have 5 minutes left to complete this section."

4. Maintain a realistic test-taking environment by not allowing talking, eating, outside notes, or the use of any electronic devices during the section.

5. Discuss the answers using the answer key on page 934.

View full answer explanations at:

ivyglobal.com/teach

HOMEWORK

At the end of class, answer any questions and assign the homework:

Hours 49-50	
Assignment	Page(s)
Complete a timed essay in 50 minutes using prompt #4	444-445

HOURS 51-52
READING PRACTICE

Task	Materials (All Pages in New SAT Guide)	Time
Homework Review		5 minutes
Vocabulary quiz	Pgs. 227-239	10 minutes
Reading Passage Types Review	Pgs. 72-106	15 minutes
Break		10 minutes
Reading Practice Set	Pgs. 893-905; 934	1 hour 20 minutes
Essay Marking	Pgs. 424-426	After class

HOMEWORK REVIEW (5 MINUTES)

1. Use this time to review any questions or exercises that students had trouble with, or to quiz students on what strategies or information they read about in the New SAT Guide.

2. Also collect the timed 50-minute essay that students completed for homework.

VOCABULARY QUIZ (10 MINUTES)

1. Spend 10 minutes quizzing your class on the roots, prefixes, and suffixes they previously learned for homework, along with words from the vocabulary list. You can call or write out roots or vocabulary words that students must identify either individually or in teams. You can also have students compose sentences using vocabulary words, or give examples of words that use certain roots, prefixes, and suffixes. See *Classroom Advice* for more ideas and information.

2. You can also give students a written quiz to complete. As an owner of this book you can download quizzes on roots, prefixes, suffixes, and vocabulary words for your use.

Download handouts (PDF) at:

ivyglobal.com/teach

3. You can also complete the vocabulary quiz at another point during your class session, such as halfway through, to help break up other material and provide variety.

READING PASSAGE TYPES REVIEW (15 MINUTES)

1. Review the different types of reading passages using pages 72-106 for reference. Review the special features of each type of passages, as well as the distinct strategies and approach to use for each one. Also make sure students understand how many of each passage type they will encounter.

2. You can call on students to list the unique features of each type of passage, or have them write them on a whiteboard or blackboard, or discuss them in groups.

BREAK (10 MINUTES)

READING PRACTICE SET (1 HOUR 20 MINUTES)

1. Give students 65 minutes to complete the full Reading Section from the second full Practice Test on pages 893-905.

2. Ensure there is a way for students to keep track of time. If there is no easily visible clock where you are teaching, you can run a countdown timer through a projection screen or mark the time remaining on a whiteboard or chalkboard.

3. Give your students a verbal 5-minute warning when they have 5 minutes left in the section. Say: "You now have 5 minutes left to complete this section."

4. Maintain a realistic test-taking environment by not allowing talking, eating, outside notes, or the use of any electronic devices during the section.

173

5. Discuss the answers using the answer key on page 934 and the full answer explanations.

> Download handouts (PDF) at:
>
> ivyglobal.com/teach

ESSAY MARKING (AFTER CLASS)

1. Before the next class session mark each student's essay using the College Board's rubric provided on pages 424-426. Provide a score of 1-4 in each of Reading, Analysis, and Writing, with notes if applicable.

2. Provide comments on how to improve where appropriate, and indicate any relevant parts of the essay that demonstrate good work or could be edited. You may also note any issues with grammar, spelling, or diction.

HOMEWORK

At the end of class, answer any questions and assign the homework:

Hours 51-52	
Assignment	Page(s)
Review all math concepts from previous chapters in preparation for covering new content	482-647
Memorize the remaining 9 suffixes; Memorize Vocabulary words 141-160	230; 235-236

Hours 53-54

Math: Additional Topics

Task	Materials (All Pages in New SAT Guide)	Time
Homework Review	Pgs. 482-647; 230; 235-236	5 minutes
Vocabulary quiz	Pgs. 227-239	10 minutes
Introductory Geometry	Pgs. 735-756	45 minutes
Break		10 minutes
Right Triangles	Pgs. 757-768	25 minutes
Radians and the Unit Circle	Pgs. 769-780	25 minutes

Homework Review (5 minutes)

1. Use this time to review any questions or exercises that students had trouble with, or to quiz students on what strategies or information they read about in the New SAT Guide.

Vocabulary Quiz (10 minutes)

1. Spend 10 minutes quizzing your class on the roots, prefixes, and suffixes they previously learned for homework, along with words from the vocabulary list. You can call or write out roots or vocabulary words that students must identify either individually or in teams. You can also have students compose sentences using vocabulary words, or give examples of words that use certain roots, prefixes, and suffixes. See *Classroom Advice* for more ideas and information.

2. You can also give students a written quiz to complete. As an owner of this book you can download quizzes on roots, prefixes, suffixes, and vocabulary words for your use.

3. You can also complete the vocabulary quiz at another point during your class session, such as halfway through, to help break up other material and provide variety.

INTRODUCTORY GEOMETRY (45 MINUTES)

1. Cover the material on pages 735-752 on Additional Topics in math, and the first category of introductory geometry. Make sure students understand the basic properties of lines, angles, and the various shapes covered in the section.

2. Give students 10 minutes to complete the practice questions on pages 752-754. Discuss the answers using the answer key on page 756.

BREAK (10 MINUTES)

RIGHT TRIANGLES (25 MINUTES)

1. Cover the material on pages 757-764 on right triangles. Make sure students understand how to use the Pythagorean Theorem, special triangles, and trigonometry.

2. Give students 10 minutes to complete the practice questions on pages 764-766. Discuss the answers using the answer key on page 768.

RADIANS AND THE UNIT CIRCLE (25 MINUTES)

1. Cover the material on radians and the unit circle on pages 769-777. Make sure students understand how to measure angles using radians, as discussed on pages 769-770, as well as using the unit circle to solve problems.

2. Give students 12 minutes to complete the practice questions on pages 777-778. Discuss the answers using the answer key on page 780.

HOMEWORK

At the end of class, answer any questions and assign the homework:

Hours 53-54	
Assignment	Page(s)
Complete questions #1-14 from Additional Topics practice set	797-802
Memorize Vocabulary words 161-180	236-237

HOURS 55-56
MATH: ADDITIONAL TOPICS + ESSAY PRACTICE

Task	Materials (All Pages in New SAT Guide)	Time
Homework Review	Pgs. 797-802; 236-237	5 minutes
Vocabulary quiz	Pgs. 227-239	10 minutes
Circles	Pgs. 781-790; Circles Worksheet	25 minutes
Complex Numbers	Pgs. 791-796	20 minutes
Break		10 minutes
Essay Practice	Pgs. 442-443	50 minutes
Essay Marking	Pgs. 424-426	After class

HOMEWORK REVIEW (5 MINUTES)

1. Use this time to review any questions or exercises that students had trouble with, or to quiz students on what strategies or information they read about in the New SAT Guide.

VOCABULARY QUIZ (10 MINUTES)

1. Spend 10 minutes quizzing your class on the roots, prefixes, and suffixes they previously learned for homework, along with words from the vocabulary list. You can call or write out roots or vocabulary words that students must identify either individually or in teams. You can also have students compose sentences using vocabulary words, or give examples of words that use certain roots, prefixes, and suffixes. See *Classroom Advice* for more ideas and information.

2. You can also give students a written quiz to complete. As an owner of this book you can download quizzes on roots, prefixes, suffixes, and vocabulary words for your use.

3. You can also complete the vocabulary quiz at another point during your class session, such as halfway through, to help break up other material and provide variety.

CIRCLES (25 MINUTES)

1. Cover the material on pages 781-786 on circles. Make sure students understand chords, arcs, and sectors, as well as how to graph circles as explained on pages 785-786.

2. Give students 12 minutes to complete the practice questions on pages 787-789. Discuss the answers using the answer key on page 790.

3. For additional practice, you can also have students complete the Circles Worksheet, or assign it for homework.

COMPLEX NUMBERS (20 MINUTES)

1. Cover the material on pages 791-795 on complex numbers. Make sure students understand both imaginary and complex numbers.

2. Give students 10 minutes to complete the practice questions on page 795. Discuss the answers using the answer key on page 796.

3. For additional practice, you can also have students complete the Complex Numbers Worksheet, or assign it for homework.

BREAK (10 MINUTES)

ESSAY PRACTICE (50 MINUTES)

1. Give students 50 minutes to write an essay using Essay Prompt #4 on pages 442-443. Students can write on a loose sheet of paper, which you will collect at the end.

2. Ensure there is a way for students to keep track of time. If there is no easily visible clock where you are teaching, you can run a countdown timer through a projection screen or mark the time remaining on a whiteboard or chalkboard.

3. Give your students a verbal 5-minute warning when they have 5 minutes left to finish their essays. Say: "You now have 5 minutes left to complete this section."

ESSAY MARKING (AFTER CLASS)

1. Before the next class session mark each student's essay using the College Board's rubric provided on pages 424-426. Provide a score of 1-4 in each of Reading, Analysis, and Writing, with notes if applicable.

2. Provide comments on how to improve where appropriate, and indicate any relevant parts of the essay that demonstrate good work or could be edited. You may also note any issues with grammar, spelling, or diction.

HOMEWORK

At the end of class, answer any questions and assign the homework:

Hours 55-56	
Assignment	Page(s)
Complete questions #15-30 to finish Additional Topics practice set	803-807
Memorize Vocabulary words 181-200	237

HOURS 57-60
DIAGNOSTIC TEST

Task	Materials	Time
Proctor Diagnostic Test	Practice Test #1	4 hours
Prepare Score Report	Diagnostic Analysis Scoring Sheet	After class

PROCTOR DIAGNOSTIC TEST (4 HOURS)

1. Proctor a full-length diagnostic SAT for your class. Use the first practice test from either 5 Practice Tests (Ivy Global) or Official Study Guide for the New SAT (College Board). Students must complete the sections in the order they are given, and can only work on one section at a time. The test sections always appear in the same order:

   - 65-minute Reading section
   - 25-minute No-calculator Math section
     o 5-minute Break
   - 35-minute Writing section
   - 55-minute Calculator Math section
     o 5-minute Break
   - 50-minute Essay

2. Provide a 5-minute break after the No-calculator Math section, and after the Calculator Math section if your students will be completing the Essay section.

3. Let the students know the order of test sections and breaks. Let students know that there is no penalty for wrong answers, so they are encouraged to guess on any questions they cannot complete. Students must mark down their answers on their bubble sheets, and not just in their test booklets.

4. Ensure there is a way for students to keep track of time. If there is no easily visible clock where you are teaching, you can run a countdown timer through a projection screen or mark the time remaining on a whiteboard or chalkboard.

5. Always give your students a verbal 5-minute warning when they have 5 minutes left in the section. Say: "You now have 5 minutes left to complete this section."

6. Maintain a realistic test-taking environment by not allowing talking, eating, outside notes, or the use of any electronic devices during the test. Students may use a calculator, including scientific or graphing calculator, during the Calculator Math section only.

7. Be sure students complete their test with an HB or #2 pencil. Pen marks will not show up on the SAT test and students could receive no credit for their answers or essay.

8. If this is your final class session, inform students that their scores will be sent to them within a few days. You can email student scores and/or make them available for pick-up by students and parents. See *Classroom Advice* for more information on diagnostics.

9. If this is not your final class session, aim to have Score Reports prepared to return to your students at the next class session if possible.

Download printable answer sheets (PDF) at:
ivyglobal.com/teach

PREPARE SCORE REPORT (AFTER CLASS)

1. Follow the instructions on the Diagnostic Analysis Scoring Sheet to prepare a Score Report for each student. You will complete this after the class.

2. Send out Score Reports for students or make them available for pick-up if your course is complete. Return Score Reports during your next class session if your class will continue.

SECTION 7
72-HOUR COURSE CURRICULUM

The 72-hour course consists of the following curriculum pages built on top of the previous 12-hour, 24-hour, 36-hour, 48-hour, and 60-hour courses. To complete the full 72-hour course first work through hours 1-60 from those courses, and then continue with the following pages to work through hours 61-72.

HOURS 61-62

Task	Materials	Time
Homework Review		5 minutes
Reading Practice	Practice Test #2	75 minutes
Break		10 minutes
No-Calculator Math Practice	Practice Test #2	30 minutes

HOMEWORK REVIEW (5 MINUTES)

1. Use this time to review any questions or exercises that students had trouble with, or to quiz students on vocabulary words and roots, prefixes, and suffixes from the New SAT Guide.

READING PRACTICE (75 MINUTES)

1. Give students 65 minutes to complete the full Reading Section from Practice Test #2 in either 5 Practice Tests (Ivy Global) or Official Study Guide for the New SAT (College Board).

2. Ensure there is a way for students to keep track of time. If there is no easily visible clock where you are teaching, you can run a countdown timer through a projection screen or mark the time remaining on a whiteboard or chalkboard.

3. Give your students a verbal 5-minute warning when they have 5 minutes left in the section. Say: "You now have 5 minutes left to complete this section."

4. Maintain a realistic test-taking environment by not allowing talking, eating, outside notes, or the use of any electronic devices during the section.

5. Discuss the answers for 10 minutes using the answer key.

BREAK (10 MINUTES)

NO-CALCULATOR MATH PRACTICE (30 MINUTES)

1. Give students 25 minutes to complete the full No-Calculator Math Section from Practice Test #2 in either 5 Practice Tests (Ivy Global) or Official Study Guide for the New SAT (College Board).

2. Ensure there is a way for students to keep track of time. If there is no easily visible clock where you are teaching, you can run a countdown timer through a projection screen or mark the time remaining on a whiteboard or chalkboard.

3. Give your students a verbal 5-minute warning when they have 5 minutes left in the section. Say: "You now have 5 minutes left to complete this section."

4. Maintain a realistic test-taking environment by not allowing talking, eating, outside notes, or the use of any electronic devices during the section.

5. Discuss the answers for 5 minutes using the answer key.

HOMEWORK

At the end of class, answer any questions and assign the homework:

Hours 61-62	
Assignment	Page(s)
Complete a timed 50-minute essay using the prompt from Practice Test #2	Practice Test #2

Hours 63-64

Writing + Math Practice

Task	Materials	Time
Homework Review	Practice Test #2 – Essay Prompt	5 minutes
Writing Practice	Practice Test #2	40 minutes
Break		10 minutes
Calculator Math Practice	Practice Test #2	65 minutes

Homework Review (5 minutes)

1. Use this time to discuss the prompt that students responded to for their essay, or to quiz students on strategies for approaching the essay.

Writing Practice (40 minutes)

1. Give students 35 minutes to complete the full Writing Section from Practice Test #2 in either 5 Practice Tests (Ivy Global) or Official Study Guide for the New SAT (College Board).

2. Ensure there is a way for students to keep track of time. If there is no easily visible clock where you are teaching, you can run a countdown timer through a projection screen or mark the time remaining on a whiteboard or chalkboard.

3. Give your students a verbal 5-minute warning when they have 5 minutes left in the section. Say: "You now have 5 minutes left to complete this section."

4. Maintain a realistic test-taking environment by not allowing talking, eating, outside notes, or the use of any electronic devices during the section.

5. Discuss the answers for 5 minutes using the answer key.

BREAK (10 MINUTES)

CALCULATOR MATH PRACTICE (65 MINUTES)

1. Give students 55 minutes to complete the full Calculator Math Section from Practice Test #2 in either 5 Practice Tests (Ivy Global) or Official Study Guide for the New SAT (College Board).

2. Ensure there is a way for students to keep track of time. If there is no easily visible clock where you are teaching, you can run a countdown timer through a projection screen or mark the time remaining on a whiteboard or chalkboard.

3. Give your students a verbal 5-minute warning when they have 5 minutes left in the section. Say: "You now have 5 minutes left to complete this section."

4. Maintain a realistic test-taking environment by not allowing talking, eating, outside notes, or the use of any electronic devices during the section.

5. Discuss the answers for 10 minutes using the answer key.

HOMEWORK

At the end of class, answer any questions and assign the homework:

Hours 63-64	
Assignment	Page(s)
Students can score Practice Test #2	Practice Test #2
Take time to analyze questions they could not answer or answered incorrectly in each section, identify the type of question, and review the relevant material in the New SAT Guide	For example, if students missed questions on probability, review pages 681-697. If they had problems with paired passages, review pages 101-102 and 191-194

HOURS 65-66
READING + MATH PRACTICE

Task	Materials	Time
Homework Review	Practice Test #2	5 minutes
Reading Practice	Practice Test #3	75 minutes
Break		10 minutes
No-Calculator Math Practice	Practice Test #3	30 minutes

HOMEWORK REVIEW (5 MINUTES)

1. Use this time to review any questions or exercises that students had trouble with.

READING PRACTICE (75 MINUTES)

1. Give students 65 minutes to complete the full Reading Section from Practice Test #3 in either 5 Practice Tests (Ivy Global) or Official Study Guide for the New SAT (College Board).

2. Ensure there is a way for students to keep track of time. If there is no easily visible clock where you are teaching, you can run a countdown timer through a projection screen or mark the time remaining on a whiteboard or chalkboard.

3. Give your students a verbal 5-minute warning when they have 5 minutes left in the section. Say: "You now have 5 minutes left to complete this section."

4. Maintain a realistic test-taking environment by not allowing talking, eating, outside notes, or the use of any electronic devices during the section.

5. Discuss the answers for 10 minutes using the answer key.

View full answer explanations at:

ivyglobal.com/teach

BREAK (10 MINUTES)

NO-CALCULATOR MATH PRACTICE (30 MINUTES)

1. Give students 25 minutes to complete the full No-Calculator Math Section from Practice Test #3 in either 5 Practice Tests (Ivy Global) or Official Study Guide for the New SAT (College Board).

2. Ensure there is a way for students to keep track of time. If there is no easily visible clock where you are teaching, you can run a countdown timer through a projection screen or mark the time remaining on a whiteboard or chalkboard.

3. Give your students a verbal 5-minute warning when they have 5 minutes left in the section. Say: "You now have 5 minutes left to complete this section."

4. Maintain a realistic test-taking environment by not allowing talking, eating, outside notes, or the use of any electronic devices during the section.

5. Discuss the answers for 5 minutes using the answer key.

View full answer explanations at:

ivyglobal.com/teach

HOMEWORK

At the end of class, answer any questions and assign the homework:

Hours 65-66	
Assignment	Page(s)
Complete the Calculator math section from Practice Test #3, timed for 55 minutes	Practice Test #3

HOURS 67-68

ESSAY + WRITING PRACTICE

Task	Materials *(All Pages in New SAT Guide)*	Time
Homework Review	Practice Test #3	5 minutes
Essay Practice	Practice Test #3	60 minutes
Break		10 minutes
Writing Practice	Practice Test #3	45 minutes
Essay Marking	Pgs. 242-246	After Class

HOMEWORK REVIEW (5 MINUTES)

1. Use this time to review any questions that students had trouble with.

ESSAY PRACTICE (60 MINUTES)

1. Give students 50 minutes to write an essay using the prompt from Practice Test #3 in either 5 Practice Tests (Ivy Global) or Official Study Guide for the New SAT (College Board).

2. Ensure there is a way for students to keep track of time. If there is no easily visible clock where you are teaching, you can run a countdown timer through a projection screen or mark the time remaining on a whiteboard or chalkboard.

3. Give your students a verbal 5-minute warning when they have 5 minutes left in the section. Say: "You now have 5 minutes left to complete this section."

4. Maintain a realistic test-taking environment by not allowing talking, eating, outside notes, or the use of any electronic devices during the section.

5. Discuss the essay prompt and how students responded to it for 10 minutes. Collect the essays, making sure students have included their names.

BREAK (10 MINUTES)

WRITING PRACTICE (45 MINUTES)

1. Give students 35 minutes to complete the Writing Section from Practice Test #3 in either 5 Practice Tests (Ivy Global) or Official Study Guide for the New SAT (College Board).

2. Ensure there is a way for students to keep track of time. If there is no easily visible clock where you are teaching, you can run a countdown timer through a projection screen or mark the time remaining on a whiteboard or chalkboard.

3. Give your students a verbal 5-minute warning when they have 5 minutes left in the section. Say: "You now have 5 minutes left to complete this section."

4. Maintain a realistic test-taking environment by not allowing talking, eating, outside notes, or the use of any electronic devices during the section.

5. Discuss the answers for 10 minutes using the answer key.

View full answer explanations at:
ivyglobal.com/teach

HOMEWORK

At the end of class, answer any questions and assign the homework:

Hours 67-68	
Assignment	Page(s)
Review the approach/strategies for all sections, focusing on areas of difficulty. At a minimum it would be helpful to review notes taken during class, and the pages on approaching each section of the test	Reading pgs. 33-58; Writing pgs. 262-279; Essay pgs. 391-398; Math pgs. 455-476.
Students should prepare everything the way they would before they take the SAT. This includes bringing all necessary materials (appropriate pencils, calculator, snacks etc.) and having a 'dry run' of their routine for test day	

HOURS 69-72

Task	Materials	Time
Proctor Diagnostic Test	Practice Test #4	4 hours
Prepare Score Report	Diagnostic Analysis Scoring Sheet	After class

PROCTOR DIAGNOSTIC TEST (4 HOURS)

1. Proctor a full-length diagnostic SAT for your class. Use the fourth practice test from either 5 Practice Tests (Ivy Global) or Official Study Guide for the New SAT (College Board). Students must complete the sections in the order they are given, and can only work on one section at a time. The test sections always appear in the same order:

   - 65-minute Reading section
   - 25-minute No-calculator Math section
     - o 5-minute Break
   - 35-minute Writing section
   - 55-minute Calculator Math section
     - o 5-minute Break
   - 50-minute Essay

2. Provide a 5-minute break after the No-calculator Math section, and after the Calculator Math section if your students will be completing the Essay section.

3. Let the students know the order of test sections and breaks. Let students know that there is no penalty for wrong answers, so they are encouraged to guess on any questions they cannot complete. Students must mark down their answers on their bubble sheets, and not just in their test booklets.

4. Ensure there is a way for students to keep track of time. If there is no easily visible clock where you are teaching, you can run a countdown timer through a projection screen or mark the time remaining on a whiteboard or chalkboard.

5. Always give your students a verbal 5-minute warning when they have 5 minutes left in the section. Say: "You now have 5 minutes left to complete this section."

6. Maintain a realistic test-taking environment by not allowing talking, eating, outside notes, or the use of any electronic devices during the test. Students may use a calculator, including scientific or graphing calculator, during the Calculator Math section only.

7. Be sure students complete their test with an HB or #2 pencil. Pen marks will not show up on the SAT test and students could receive no credit for their answers or essay.

8. If this is your final class session, inform students that their scores will be sent to them within a few days. You can email student scores and/or make them available for pick-up by students and parents. See *Classroom Advice* for more information on diagnostics.

Download printable answer sheets (PDF) at:
ivyglobal.com/teach

PREPARE SCORE REPORT (AFTER CLASS)

1. Follow the instructions on the Diagnostic Analysis Scoring Sheet to prepare a Score Report for each student. You will complete this after the class.

2. Send out score reports for students or make them available for pick-up if your course is complete. Return score reports during your next class session if your class will continue.

SECTION 8
EXTENDING THE CURRICULUM

The previous pages outline a sequence of curricula that can run up to 72 hours in length. However, based on the needs of your school or company you may wish to offer a longer course. The points below offer suggestions for extending the curriculum in this Teacher's Guide to a course of 80 hours or more.

WORK MORE SLOWLY

If you are offering a longer course, you may choose to take advantage of the extra time to move more slowly through the material to be covered.

The times provided in the curricula for covering the assigned content are meant to reflect a quick-moving class that is able to stay focused and cover a lot of material. However, some groups of students may have a lot of questions or find the information covered completely novel. This is often the case with younger students, or those unfamiliar with standardized tests or common American high school material. In these instances, moving through material more slowly is a good strategy. This will ensure that your class understands everything you cover, and that no one is left behind.

If you choose to work at a slower pace, make sure that more advanced students in your class are not bored. You can offer additional or more challenging work to keep stronger students engaged and occupied. If one student is progressing at a much faster rate than the rest of the class, you can also speak to your school or company about placing them in a different class group that can provide a more appropriate challenge.

ASSIGN LESS HOMEWORK

Depending on your students' schedules and how often your class will meet, the amount of homework given throughout the course may be challenging to complete. If you are offering a longer course you have the luxury of assigning somewhat less homework to your students and covering more of that material in-class instead. This also allows students to receive more support as they work on practice questions and apply new strategies for the first time.

However, it is still important that students are assigned at least some homework to be completed between class sessions. This will keep students in the habit of engaging with SAT content frequently, rather than only thinking about it during the isolated hours that they are in class. It will also help them develop the discipline to study independently, which will bring them success on the SAT and in their college careers.

Here is an example taken from Hours 3-4 of the course. Instead of assigning both a practice set (pages 63-70) and independent reading and practice (pages 95-106), you could opt to assign only the first practice set on pages 63-70.

Hours 3-4	
Assignment	Page(s)
Complete Reading practice set	63-70
Read section on passages with graphics and complete practice sets	95-106

You would then work through the new material and practice sets on pages 95-106 together as a class during the next session, Hours 5-6. This would allow you to push back some of the content from Hours 5-6 for the following class, and thus lengthen your course.

You can also opt to have your students complete a review of the day's lesson for homework, and ensure their compliance by quizzing them on the strategies and content they should have reviewed. This will leave you more time to complete practice questions during class, where you can monitor and support your students.

More Homework Review

Another way to adjust the homework in a longer course is to offer more time for homework review. If your class will be completing a lot of practice sections on their own, reviewing any challenging questions can be a great benefit to them. You can spend time reviewing not only how to reach the correct response for individual questions, but also what approach to use to solve problems in different parts of the test.

You can also employ more interactive forms of homework review with your students when you have more time. Have your students engage in discussion about what they read, or invite students to explain how they tackled a tough question by describing their process or showing their work on a whiteboard or chalkboard.

You may opt to set aside 10 to 15 minutes for homework review in every 2-hour session, or to be flexible based on the needs of your class.

More Vocabulary Review

Similar to allocating more time for homework review, you may decide to spend more time with your class on interactive vocabulary review. This might take the form of team-based competition or even individual written quizzes. This is a good option for classes composed mainly of younger students, or students whose first language is not English.

You may opt to set aside 10 or 15 minutes for vocabulary review in every 2-hour session, or to set aside a larger amount of time every few classes for a thorough review or game. Remember that you can download and print vocabulary quizzes to be used in your classes.

Download quizzes (PDF) at:
ivyglobal.com/teach

DIAGNOSTIC REVIEW

Another way to extend and enrich your curriculum is to add time for review of all diagnostic tests. You can take up difficult questions as a class, and discuss what strategies and approaches can be used for each question. This is a great way for students to see course content in action and review key concepts.

If you wish to offer a final diagnostic test for your students beyond the 72-hour course, you can use Practice Test 5 from 5 Practice Tests (Ivy Global) or a practice test from Official Study Guide for the New SAT (College Board).

REVIEW CHALLENGING CONTENT

In a long course, review not only becomes possible but necessary, so that students do not forget content they learned early on by the end of the course. Reviewing previously covered topics allows students to retain more information, as well as clarify any concepts they did not fully understand the first time around.

Grammar is one topic that is important to review. Many students receive little or no grammar instruction during high school, so some of the concepts covered in the SAT curricula may be entirely new to them. Many correct constructions may also feel counterintuitive when students first encounter them. Thus, review is necessary to change old habits and help students learn to spot unfamiliar errors.

Math is another area that warrants additional review. Even though the math topics covered have been pared down on the new SAT, students still need to know a fairly wide range of content. Frequent review can reinforce these key concepts so students have the mastery of information they need to tackle difficult problems.

REPEAT HELPFUL DRILLS

Finally, beyond reviewing content you may also decide to repeat exercises that were beneficial to your class. For example, it may be helpful for many students to repeat the Essay-writing drill from Hours 31-32, where students compose an essay in sections, pausing to discuss each one before continuing. Pay attention during your course to any exercise or drill that is particularly useful to your students, so you can return to it again as necessary.

Chapter 3
Private Tutoring

SECTION 1
TUTORING SYLLABI

These pages contain syllabi for all the tutoring curricula that follow. They provide a snapshot of each outline that you can refer to while planning your sessions or working with your student.

8-Hour Tutoring

Part 1

Hours 1-2: Introduction to the SAT & Reading Test

Instruction Time		
Task	Materials *(All Pages in New SAT Guide)*	Time
Get to know your student		5 minutes
Introduction to the SAT	Pgs. 6-20	30 minutes
Introduction to Vocabulary Building	Pgs. 227-231	10 minutes
Introduction to Reading Comprehension	Pgs. 29-32	5 minutes
Reading a Passage	Pgs. 34-46	30 minutes
Reading Questions & Selecting Answers	Pgs. 47-62	40 minutes

Homework	
Assignment	Page(s)
Memorize the first 15 roots (to *civi*)	227-228
Memorize vocabulary words 1-20	231
Complete Reading practice set	63-70
Read section and complete practice sets	95-106

Hours 3-4: Introduction to Writing & Math

Instruction Time		
Task	Materials *(All Pages in New SAT Guide)*	Time
Homework Review	Pgs. 227-228; 213; 63-70; 95-106	15 minutes
Introduction to Writing	Pgs. 257-261	5 minutes
Reading the Passages	Pgs. 263-268	5 minutes
Reading Questions & Selecting Answers	Pgs. 269-282	25 minutes
SAT Grammar	Pgs. 283-302	30 minutes
Introduction to Math	Pgs. 451-454	5 minutes
Approaching Math	Pgs. 456-476	35 minutes

Homework	
Assignment	Page(s)
Memorize roots 16-25 (to *locqu*)	228
Memorize vocabulary words 21-40	231-232
Read and complete writing practice set	303-314
Complete math practice set	477-479
Complete math practice set and note difficult questions for review	503-507

Hours 5-6: Math Review + Introduction to the Essay

Instruction Time		
Task	Materials *(All Pages in New SAT Guide)*	Time
Homework Review	Pgs. 228; 231-232; 303-314; 447-479; 503-507	15 minutes
Fundamental Math Review	Pgs. 482-502	15 minutes
Heart of Algebra Review	Pgs. 508-544	30 minutes
Introduction to the Essay	Pgs. 387-390	5 minutes
Approaching the Essay	Pgs. 392-400	20 minutes
Analyzing Arguments	Pgs. 415-420	15 minutes
Rubric & Sample Essay	Pgs. 424-428; 430-432; 434-436	20 minutes

Homework	
Assignment	Page(s)
Memorize roots 26-35 (to *pac*)	228
Complete a 50-minute practice essay using Sample Prompt #1	437-439
All remaining practice questions from Heart of Algebra review	508-544

HOURS 7-8: ALL SECTIONS + CREATING A STUDY SCHEDULE

Instruction Time		
Task	Materials *(All Pages in New SAT Guide)*	Time
Homework Review	Pgs. 228; 437-439; 509-544	15 minutes
Essay Marking	Pgs. 424-426	During session
Reading Passage Types	Pgs. 72-87	30 minutes
Harder Grammar Errors	Pgs. 315-322	30 minutes
Heart of Algebra Review Continued	Pgs. 545-576	30 minutes
Creating a Study Schedule	Pgs. 21-23	15 minutes

Homework	
Assignment	Page(s)
Memorize roots 36-45 (to *spec*)	228-229
Memorize vocabulary words 41-60	232-233
Literature and science practice passages	77-80; 87-88
Harder Grammar Error practice	323-324
Grammar section review	325-326
All remaining practice questions from Heart of Algebra review	545-576
Heart of Algebra practice set	577-586
Review returned essay comments	

12-HOUR TUTORING
PART 2

HOURS 9-10: READING PASSAGE TYPES + WRITING PASSAGES

Instruction Time		
Task	Materials *(All Pages in New SAT Guide)*	Time
Homework Review	Pgs. 228-229; 77-80; 87-88; 323-326; 577-586	15 minutes
Reading Passage Types Continued	Pgs. 87-106	45 minutes
Expressing Ideas	Pgs. 335-366	60 minutes

Homework	
Assignment	Page(s)
Memorize final 7 roots	229
Memorize vocabulary words 61-80	233
Complete social science & history, graphics, and paired passages practice	93-94; 98-100; 104-106
Complete two reading practice passages, aiming to complete them in under 25 minutes	240-245
Expressing Ideas practice set	267-274

HOURS 11-12: ADVANCED MATH + ANALYZING ESSAY PROMPTS

Instruction Time		
Task	Materials *(All Pages in New SAT Guide)*	Time
Homework Review	Pgs. 229; 93-94; 98-100; 104-106; 240-245; 267-274	15 minutes
Passport to Advanced Math	Pgs. 587-636	60 minutes
Analyzing an Argument	Pgs. 401-415	30 minutes
Essay Practice	Pgs. 440-441	15 minutes

Homework	
Assignment	Page(s)
Memorize prefixes 1-10 (to *extro*)	229
Memorize vocabulary words 81-100	233-234
All remaining questions from Passport to Advanced Math review	587-636
Passport to Advanced Math practice set	637-646
Complete essay outline for Prompt #2	440-441

16-Hour Tutoring

Part 3

Hours 13-14: Reading Question Types + Math Problem Solving

	Instruction Time	
Task	Materials *(All Pages in New SAT Guide)*	Time
Homework Review	Pgs. 229; 233-234; 587-636; 637-646; 440-441	15 minutes
Understanding the Facts questions	Pgs. 108-142	60 minutes
Problem Solving and Data Analysis	Pgs. 647-722	45 minutes

Homework	
Assignment	Page(s)
Memorize prefixes 11-20 (to *post*)	229-230
Understanding the Facts practice set	143-150
All remaining questions from Problem Solving and Data Analysis review	647-722
Problem Solving and Data Analysis practice set	723-734

Hours 15-16: Grammar Review + Essay Practice

	Instruction Time	
Task	Materials *(All Pages in New SAT Guide)*	Time
Homework Review	Pgs. 229-230; 143-150; 647-722; 723-734	15 minutes
Grammar Review	Pgs. 283-324; Common Grammar Errors worksheet; Confused Words & Idioms quiz;	15 minutes
Grammar practice set	Pgs. 327-332	30 minutes
Essay practice	Pgs. 442-443	60 minutes

Homework	
Assignment	Page(s)
Memorize final 8 prefixes	230
Memorize words 101-120	234-235
Reading Practice Section timed	240-252
Math Practice Section timed	822-827

20-HOUR TUTORING OUTLINE
PART 4

HOURS 17-18: READING QUESTION TYPES + ADDITIONAL TOPICS IN MATH

Instruction Time		
Task	Materials *(All Pages in New SAT Guide)*	Time
Homework Review	Pgs. 230; 234-235; 240-252; 822-827	15 minutes
Persuasive Language questions	Pgs. 152-180	45 minutes
Additional Topics in Math	Pgs. 735-796	60 minutes

Homework	
Assignment	Page(s)
Memorize first 10 suffixes (to *-ful*)	230
Memorize words 121-140	234-235
Persuasive Language practice set	181-188
All remaining questions from Additional Topics review	735-796
Additional Topics practice set	797-807

HOURS 19-20: WRITING & ESSAY PRACTICE + TEST DAY PREP

Instruction Time		
Task	Materials *(All Pages in New SAT Guide)*	Time
Homework Review	Pgs. 230; 234-235; 181-188; 735-796; 797-807	15 minutes
Writing Practice Section	375-382; 384	45 minutes
Essay practice	444-445	30 minutes
Test day approach and review	24-26	30 minutes

Homework	
Assignment	Page(s)
Memorize the remaining 10 suffixes	230
Memorize words 141-160	235-236
Complete the remainder of Sample Prompt #4 essay	444-445
Complete a 50-minute practice essay using Sample Prompt #5	446-447
Math practice section timed	809-818

SECTION 2
8-HOUR TUTORING CURRICULUM

The following pages provide an 8-hour curriculum for one-on-one or small group tutoring, which you can adapt as necessary to suit the needs of your student(s).

HOURS 1-2
INTRODUCTION TO THE SAT & READING TEST

Task	Materials *(All Pages in New SAT Guide)*	Time
Get to know your student		5 minutes
Introduction to the SAT	Pgs. 6-20	30 minutes
Introduction to Vocabulary Building	Pgs. 227-231	10 minutes
Introduction to Reading Comprehension	Pgs. 29-32	5 minutes
Reading a Passage	Pgs. 34-46	30 minutes
Reading Questions & Selecting Answers	Pgs. 47-62	40 minutes

GET TO KNOW YOUR STUDENT (5 MINUTES)

1. Take a few minutes to introduce yourself to your student, and ask them to introduce themselves. Ask your student about what subjects he or she likes in school, their goals for the SAT, and prior experience with the SAT or PSAT. You can also ask other questions about things like extracurricular interests. Your goal is to help your student feel comfortable and get to know them.

2. Take time to explain any policies you have such as expectations around homework, and what materials your student needs to bring to sessions. At a minimum, your student should bring their New SAT Guide, pencils, paper, and a calculator to every tutoring session.

INTRODUCTION TO THE SAT (30 MINUTES)

1. Introduce your student to the basics of the SAT test. Use pages 6-11 to discuss what the SAT is and why it matters, as well as changes for the new SAT as explained on page 8. Make sure your student understands the format of the new exam as detailed on page 9, as well as the new SAT scoring explained in the chart on page 10.

2. Next, use pages 12-14 to explain how to plan for taking the SAT. Make sure your student understands the need to plan ahead and register early for his or her test date, especially if he or she would like to apply for Early Admission as explained on page 13.

3. Use pages 15-20 to discuss general pointers for approaching the SAT. Make sure your student understands how a standardized test is different from most school exams as discussed on page 16, and the importance of managing time effectively using the ideas on page 17. Also remind your student that there is no penalty for wrong answers, and walk them through how to make an educated guess using the example on page 19.

4. If your student has already taken a diagnostic test, you can also use this time to discuss their results and set goals for improvement.

INTRODUCTION TO VOCABULARY BUILDING (10 MINUTES)

1. Discuss the importance of vocabulary to the Reading and Writing Tests using page 227. Mention how vocabulary plays a different role on the new SAT, as it is not tested directly except for questions about words used in context in Reading passages. Thus, there will be less focus on memorizing individual words and more on understanding roots, prefixes, and suffixes, and on mastering other portions of the Reading and Writing Test.

2. Introduce the concepts of roots, prefixes, and suffixes, using pages 227-230. Discuss a few roots, prefixes, and suffixes and how their meaning is demonstrated by words that contain them. Emphasize that learning these word parts provides a great return on your student's time investment, as it will help him or her recognize lots of new words, and thus is generally more useful and efficient than memorizing large numbers of vocabulary words.

3. Introduce your student to the vocabulary list on page 231. Suggest that your student learn the words by making flashcards, writing them down in sentences, or using them in conversation with family and friends. You can give examples of how some of the vocabulary words could be used in context. Remind your student that while

learning vocabulary words is useful, it should not be the focus of his or her efforts. There will be time for vocabulary revision in later tutoring sessions.

INTRODUCTION TO READING COMPREHENSION (5 MINUTES)

1. Introduce your student to the content and format of the new SAT Reading Test by covering the material on pages 29-32.

2. Make sure your student understands that he or she will have 65 minutes for the entire section, and there will be 5 passages, as explained in the chart on page 31.

READING A PASSAGE (30 MINUTES)

1. Cover the material on pages 34-38 about how to read and mark up an SAT Passage.

2. Then, give your student 5 minutes to mark up the rest of the sample passage given on page 39. Afterwards, discuss what items your student underlined while referencing the fully marked-up passage on page 40.

3. After reading about summarizing on pages 41-42, give your student 5 minutes to create summaries for the passage on pages 42-43. Afterwards, discuss your student's summaries while referencing the summaries provided on page 44.

4. Then, give your student 8 minutes to mark up and make summaries for the practice passage on page 45, and review their work after using the answer key on page 46.

READING QUESTIONS & SELECTING ANSWERS (40 MINUTES)

1. Cover the material on pages 47-49 about approaching the SAT Reading questions.

2. Then, give your student 10 minutes to complete the practice exercise on pages 50-51. Discuss the answers using the answer key on page 52.

3. Next, cover the material on pages 53-58 on selecting answers.

4. Then, give your student 12 minutes to complete the practice exercise on pages 58-60. Discuss the answers using the answer key on page 62.

HOMEWORK

At the end of your session, answer any questions and assign the homework:

Hours 1-2	
Assignment	Page(s)
Memorize the first 15 roots (to civi)	227-228
Memorize vocabulary words 1-20	231
Complete Reading practice set	63-70
Read section and complete practice sets	95-106

Hours 3-4
Introduction to Writing & Math

Task	Materials (All Pages in New SAT Guide)	Time
Homework Review	Pgs. 227-228; 213; 63-70; 95-106	15 minutes
Introduction to Writing	Pgs. 257-261	5 minutes
Reading the Passages	Pgs. 263-268	5 minutes
Reading Questions & Selecting Answers	Pgs. 269-282	25 minutes
SAT Grammar	Pgs. 283-302	30 minutes
Introduction to Math	Pgs. 451-454	5 minutes
Approaching Math	Pgs. 456-476	35 minutes

HOMEWORK REVIEW (15 MINUTES)

1. There is time included in every 2-hour tutoring block for homework review with your student. Use this time to review any questions or exercises that your student had trouble with, or to quiz your student on what strategies or information he or she read about in the New SAT Guide. See *Classroom Advice* in this guide for more ideas and information.

2. This time should also include vocabulary review, where you quiz your student on the roots, prefixes, and suffixes previously assigned for homework, along with words from the vocabulary list. You can call or write out roots or vocabulary words that your student must identify, or discuss a context in which certain words might be used. You can also have your student compose sentences using vocabulary words, or give examples of words that use certain roots, prefixes, and suffixes. See *Classroom Advice* for more ideas and information.

3. You can also complete the vocabulary quiz at another point during your tutoring session, such as halfway through, to help break up other material and provide variety.

Introduction to Writing (5 minutes)

1. Introduce your student to the content and format of the new SAT Writing Test by covering the material on pages 257-261.

2. Make sure your student understands the different kinds of passages as listed on pages 258-259, and the way questions will be presented as illustrated on pages 259-261.

Reading the Passages (5 minutes)

1. Cover the material on pages 263-265 on approaching Writing passages.

2. Then give your student 3 minutes to answer the practice questions on page 266. Discuss the answers using the answer key on page 268.

Reading Questions & Selecting Answers (25 minutes)

1. Cover the material on pages 269-271 on approaching Writing questions.

2. Then give your student 3 minutes to answer the practice questions on pages 272-273. Discuss the answers using the answer key on page 274.

3. Next, cover the material on pages 275-279 on selecting answers.

4. Then give your student 8 minutes to answer the practice questions on pages 279-280. Discuss the answers using the answer key on page 282.

SAT Grammar (30 minutes)

1. Cover the material on pages 284-286 on parts of speech.

2. Then give your student 8 minutes to answer the practice questions on pages 286-287. Discuss the answers using the answer key on page 288.

3. Next, cover the material on pages 289-299 on sentences.

4. Then give your student 8 minutes to answer the practice questions on page 300. Discuss the answers using the answer key on page 302.

INTRODUCTION TO MATH (5 MINUTES)

1. Introduce your student to the content and format of the new SAT Math Test by covering the material on pages 451-454.

2. Make sure your student understands the different topics covered as discussed on page 452, and the score breakdown of the calculator and no-calculator sections on page 454.

APPROACHING MATH (35 MINUTES)

1. Cover the material on pages 456-476 on approaching the math test and question-solving strategies. Work through the example questions on pages 465-476 together, so that your student can see them in action.

2. Ask your student about what areas of math he or she struggles with the most and observe what questions cause him or her difficulty, so you can plan to focus on those sections in future sessions.

HOMEWORK

At the end of your session, answer any questions and assign the homework:

Hours 3-4	
Assignment	Page(s)
Memorize roots 16-25 (to *locqu*)	228
Memorize vocabulary words 21-40	231-232
Read and complete writing practice set	303-314
Complete math practice set	477-479
Complete math practice set and note difficult questions for review	503-507

Hours 5-6

Math Review + Introduction to the Essay

Task	Materials (All Pages in New SAT Guide)	Time
Homework Review	Pgs. 228; 231-232; 303-314; 447-479; 503-507	15 minutes
Fundamental Math Review	Pgs. 482-502	15 minutes
Heart of Algebra Review	Pgs. 508-544	30 minutes
Introduction to the Essay	Pgs. 387-390	5 minutes
Approaching the Essay	Pgs. 392-400	20 minutes
Analyzing Arguments	Pgs. 415-420	15 minutes
Rubric & Sample Essay	Pgs. 424-428; 430-432; 434-436	20 minutes

Homework Review (15 minutes)

1. Use this time to review any questions or exercises that your student had trouble with, or to quiz your student on what strategies or information he or she read about in the New SAT Guide.

2. This time should also include vocabulary review, where you quiz your student on the roots, prefixes, and suffixes previously assigned for homework, along with words from the vocabulary list.

Fundamental Math Review (15 minutes)

1. Cover the material on pages 482-502 on fundamental math concepts as needed, based on what practice questions your student struggled with on pages 503-507. Make sure your student understand Properties of Integers; Factors and Multiples; Operations; Fractions; Ratios, Percentages, Proportions, and Rates; Exponents; Radicals; and Scientific Notation.

2. Work through the example questions in each topic, so that your student can see how to use these concepts to find solutions.

HEART OF ALGEBRA REVIEW (25 MINUTES)

1. Cover the material on pages 508-544 on heart of algebra concepts as needed, based on what topics your student struggles with. Make sure your student understands linear equations, inequalities, absolute value, and systems of equations and inequalities.

2. Work through a few practice questions in each topic to gauge your student's understanding. The remaining practice questions can be assigned for homework.

INTRODUCTION TO THE ESSAY (5 MINUTES)

1. Introduce your student to the new format and prompt style of the SAT Essay by covering the material on pages 387-390. Make sure your student understands the new standard prompt introduction, and the kind of passage he or she can expect to respond to.

APPROACHING THE ESSAY (20 MINUTES)

1. Cover the material on pages 392-398 on approaching the essay.

2. Then give your student 10 minutes to answer the practice questions on pages 399-400. Discuss the answers together.

ANALYZING ARGUMENTS (15 MINUTES)

1. Discuss the sample passage analysis on pages 415-418 so your student can see what to look for in a prompt passage.

2. Then discuss the identified themes from the passage on pages 418-420, so your student can see how to organize what he or she saw in the passage into themes he or she can use to write their essay.

RUBRIC & SAMPLE ESSAY (20 MINUTES)

1. Review the College Board's Rubric on pages 424-426 to show your student what their essays should contain.

2. Have your student read the sample essay prompt and passage on pages 427-428.

3. Next, review Student Sample Essay #2 on page 430, and the score breakdown on pages 431-432.

4. Next, review Student Sample Essay #4 on pages 434-435, and the score breakdown on page 436. Have a discussion with your student about what makes this a better essay than #2, and what edits he or she could make to essay #2 to receive a higher score.

HOMEWORK

At the end of your session, answer any questions and assign the homework:

Hours 5-6	
Assignment	Page(s)
Memorize roots 26-35 (to *pac*)	228
Complete a 50-minute practice essay using Sample Prompt #1	437-439
All remaining practice questions from Heart of Algebra review	508-544

Hours 7-8
All Sections + Creating a Study Schedule

Task	Materials (All Pages in New SAT Guide)	Time
Homework Review	Pgs. 228; 437-439; 509-544	15 minutes
Essay Marking	Pgs. 424-426	During session
Reading Passage Types	Pgs. 72-87	30 minutes
Harder Grammar Errors	Pgs. 315-322	30 minutes
Heart of Algebra Review Continued	Pgs. 545-576	30 minutes
Creating a Study Schedule	Pgs. 21-23	15 minutes

Homework Review (15 minutes)

1. Use this time to review any questions or exercises that your student had trouble with, or to quiz your student on what strategies or information he or she read about in the New SAT Guide.

2. This time should also include vocabulary review, where you quiz your student on the roots, prefixes, and suffixes previously assigned for homework, along with words from the vocabulary list.

Essay Marking (During Session)

1. While your student is reading or working on practice questions during your session, mark his or her essay using the College Board's rubric provided on pages 424-426. Provide a score of 1-4 in each of Reading, Analysis, and Writing, with notes if applicable.

2. Provide comments on how to improve where appropriate, and indicate any relevant parts of the essay that demonstrate good work or could be edited. You may also

note any issues with grammar, spelling, or diction. Discuss your comments with your student when you return the essay.

READING PASSAGE TYPES (30 MINUTES)

1. Discuss the different types of SAT Reading passages using page 72. Make sure your student understands that there will always be the same types of passages on each SAT test: two Social Science passages, two Science passages, and a Literature passage.

2. Cover the material on pages 73-76 on Literature passages.

3. Give your student 5 minutes to read, mark up, and make summaries for the Literature passage on page 77. Then discuss the passage together, including instances of figurative language or characterization, as well as the passage structure.

4. Cover the material on pages 81-86 on Science passages. Make sure your student understands the different elements of an argument, as explained in the chart on pages 82-83.

5. Give your student 5 minutes to read, mark up, and make summaries for the Science passage on pages 86-87. Then discuss the passage together, including its arguments and any experiments described.

HARDER GRAMMAR ERRORS (30 MINUTES)

1. Cover the material on pages 315-319 to explain parallel structure, misplaced modifiers, and logical comparison errors.

2. These grammar concepts may be new to your student, so make sure he or she sees the difference between the correct and incorrect example sentences. You can supply additional examples for your student if necessary. Some further examples are provided on the following page.

ADDITIONAL EXAMPLES OF PARALLEL STRUCTURE ERRORS:

- **Example 1:**

  - *Incorrect:* While Taylor wanted to watch the football game and have attended the housewarming event, she only had time for one activity.
  - *Correct:* While Taylor wanted to watch the football game and attend the housewarming event, she only had time for one activity.

- **Example 2:**

  - *Incorrect:* The teacher suggested that the students complete some practice tests, review the relevant chapters, and to reread their notes in preparation for the exam.
  - *Correct:* The teacher suggested that the students complete some practice tests, review the relevant chapters, and reread their notes in preparation for the exam.

ADDITIONAL EXAMPLES OF MISPLACED MODIFIER ERRORS:

- **Example 1:**

  - *Incorrect:* They carefully carried their group project to the science fair, delicate and fragile, and placed it on the table.
  - *Correct:* They carefully carried their group project, delicate and fragile, to the science fair and placed it on the table.

- **Example 2:**

  - *Incorrect:* While long and convoluted, Teresa crafted a well-researched argument in her paper that earned her the highest mark in the class.
  - *Correct:* While long and convoluted, the well-researched argument that Teresa crafted in her paper earned her the highest mark in the class.

ADDITIONAL EXAMPLES OF LOGICAL COMPARISON ERRORS:

- **Example 1:**

  - *Incorrect:* The attendees of the music festival were more boisterous than the food festival down the street.
  - *Correct:* The attendees of the music festival were more boisterous than those of the food festival down the street.

- **Example 2:**
  - *Incorrect:* The hawk's wings are much better adapted for flight than the penguin.
  - *Correct:* The hawk's wings are much better adapted for flight than the penguin's.

3. Next, discuss the commonly confused words and idioms in the charts on pages 319-322. Make sure your student understands the correct usage of the words by reviewing the example sentences, or asking your student to create their own.

4. Encourage your student to review these tables frequently until he or she has memorized the correct usage for each word. Understanding these words will also help your student when he or she writes the SAT Essay.

HEART OF ALGEBRA REVIEW CONTINUED (30 MINUTES)

1. Cover the material on pages 545-576 on the remaining Heart of Algebra concepts as needed, based on what topics your student struggles with. Make sure your student understands linear functions, interpreting equations, and graphing equations.

2. Work through a few practice questions in each topic to gauge your student's understanding. The remaining practice questions can be assigned for homework.

CREATING A STUDY SCHEDULE (15 MINUTES)

1. Discuss the importance of creating a study schedule, using pages 21-23. You can help your student begin filling in the schedule chart on page 23. If this is not your final tutoring session, you can also opt to review or work on other material, and save this discussion for your final session.

2. Encourage your student to recognize their own strengths and weaknesses based on any diagnostic tests and their homework during your sessions. He or she should aim to spend more time on his or her weakest area, while not neglecting the others.

3. To keep moving forward on any section of the test, your student can first review the content you covered together by re-reading those portions of the book. Then, he or she should keep moving through the relevant chapter by reading the content and strategies, and completing all the practice questions and drills. Also encourage your student to keep memorizing vocabulary words and roots, prefixes, and suffixes.

4. You should also present your student with specific study suggestions or homework based on the longer tutoring and curricula provided in this manual, and your observations of their progress during your sessions.

5. There are full-length practice sections at the end of each chapter that your student should use for practice. Encourage your student to attempt these sections timed, so he or she will be prepared for the time pressure of the test.

6. Encourage your student to practice with full-length diagnostics close to their test date. There are 2 complete tests in their New SAT Guide on pages 833-942 that your student can use for this purpose. Encourage them to create a realistic test-taking environment, as described on pages 831-832. He or she can score the tests himself or herself after completing them, using the instructions that follow each test.

7. Also encourage your student to read about what to expect on Test Day, including a checklist of what to bring, on pages 24-26.

HOMEWORK

At the end of your session, answer any questions and assign the homework:

Hours 7-8	
Assignment	Page(s)
Memorize roots 36-45 (to *spec*)	228-229
Memorize vocabulary words 41-60	232-233
Literature and Science practice passages	77-80; 87-88
Harder Grammar Error practice	323-324
Grammar section review	325-326
All remaining practice questions from Heart of Algebra review	545-576
Heart of Algebra practice set	577-586
Review returned essay comments	

Section 3
12-hour Tutoring Curriculum

The 12-hour tutoring curriculum consists of the following curriculum pages built on top of the previous 8-hour tutoring outline. To complete the full 12-hour tutoring curriculum, first work through hours 1-8 from the 8-hour outline, and then continue with the following pages to work through hours 9-12.

Hours 9-10
Reading Passage Types + Writing Passages

Task	Materials (All Pages in New SAT Guide)	Time
Homework Review	Pgs. 228-229; 77-80; 87-88; 323-326; 577-586	15 minutes
Reading Passage Types Continued	Pgs. 87-106	45 minutes
Expressing Ideas	Pgs. 335-366	60 minutes

HOMEWORK REVIEW (15 MINUTES)

1. Use this time to review any questions or exercises that your student had trouble with, or to quiz your student on what strategies or information he or she read about in the New SAT Guide.

2. This time should also include vocabulary review, where you quiz your student on the roots, prefixes, and suffixes previously assigned for homework, along with words from the vocabulary list.

READING PASSAGE TYPES CONTINUED (45 MINUTES)

1. Cover the material on pages 89-91 on Social Science & Historical Passages. Make sure your student understands what to expect from Founding Documents or Great Global Conversation passages, as described on page 89.

2. Give your student 5 minutes to read, mark up, and make summaries for the Founding Documents passage on page 92. Then discuss the passage together, including any rhetorical techniques. Students will answer the questions for this and the other practice passages for homework.

3. Cover the material on pages 95-96 on Passages with Graphics. Make sure your student understands the common elements in graphics, as described in the chart on pages 95-96.

4. Give your student 5 minutes to read, mark up, and make summaries for the passage and graphic on pages 96-98. Then discuss the graphic together, asking your student to identify the common elements found in the graph.

5. Cover the material on pages 101-102 on Paired Passages. Make sure your student understands the many ways that passages can be related to one another.

6. Give your student 5 minutes to read, mark up, and make summaries for the two passages on pages 103-104, breaking halfway through to discuss Passage 1 first. Then discuss both passages together, asking your student to identify the similarities and differences between the passages.

7. For example, your student should be able to spot that both passages discuss the different shift lengths that physicians-in-training have during their residency. Passage 1 suggests that longer shifts can be harmful to both patients and physicians, while Passage 2 instead argues that shorter shifts, and the "shift" mentality itself, are damaging to patients whose care is no longer the responsibility of one appointed doctor. Passage 1 cites evidence from various studies in its argument, while Passage 2 does not, instead explaining the implications of the various shift lengths. Both passages also discuss the new transition to team-based care, though they draw different conclusions about its effects. Passage 1 states that this is caused by increased specialization in medicine, and suggests the need for increased communication, while Passage 2 implies that this change is caused in part by committee regulations, and is detrimental to patient care.

EXPRESSING IDEAS (60 MINUTES)

1. Cover the material on pages 336-339 on Development of Ideas. Make sure your student understands how to identify the main point and supporting information in a passage.

2. Give your student 5 minutes to complete the practice questions on pages 339-340. Discuss the answers using the answer key on page 342.

3. Cover the material on pages 343-349 on Graphics. Make sure your student understands totals and parts, as discussed on pages 345-346.

4. Give your student 8 minutes to complete the practice questions on pages 349-350. Discuss the answers using the answer key on page 352.

5. Cover the material on pages 353-356 on Organizing Ideas. Make sure your student understands how to use the common signal words in the chart on page 355.

6. Give your student 5 minutes to complete the practice questions on pages 356-357. Discuss the answers using the answer key on page 358.

7. Cover the material on pages 359-364 on Effective Language Use. Make sure your student understands differences in style and tone as discussed on pages 362-364.

8. Give your student 5 minutes to complete the practice questions on page 365. Discuss the answers using the answer key on page 366.

HOMEWORK

At the end of your session, answer any questions and assign the homework:

Hours 9-10	
Assignment	Page(s)
Memorize final 7 roots	229
Memorize vocabulary words 61-80	233
Complete social science & history, graphics, and paired passages practice	93-94; 98-100; 104-106
Complete two reading practice passages, aiming to complete them in under 25 minutes	240-245
Expressing Ideas practice set	267-274

HOURS 11-12

ADVANCED MATH + ANALYZING ESSAY PROMPTS

Task	Materials *(All Pages in New SAT Guide)*	Time
Homework Review	Pgs. 229; 93-94; 98-100; 104-106; 240-245; 267-274	15 minutes
Passport to Advanced Math	Pgs. 587-636	60 minutes
Analyzing an Argument	Pgs. 401-415	30 minutes
Essay Practice	Pgs. 440-441	15 minutes

HOMEWORK REVIEW (15 MINUTES)

1. Use this time to review any questions or exercises that your student had trouble with, or to quiz your student on what strategies or information he or she read about in the New SAT Guide.

2. This time should also include vocabulary review, where you quiz your student on the roots, prefixes, and suffixes previously assigned for homework, along with words from the vocabulary list.

PASSPORT TO ADVANCED MATH (60 MINUTES)

1. Cover the material on pages 587-636 on Passport to Advanced Math concepts as needed, based on what topics your student struggles with. Make sure your student understands polynomial expressions, factoring polynomials, quadratic equations, quadratic functions and their graphs, advanced equations, and applications of functions.

2. Work through a few practice questions in each topic to gauge your student's understanding. The remaining practice questions can be assigned for homework.

ANALYZING AN ARGUMENT (30 MINUTES)

1. Cover the material on pages 402-404 on language use. Make sure your student understands the concept of word connotation.

2. Give your student 3 minutes to complete the first two practice questions on page 405. Discuss the answers together.

3. Cover the material on pages 406-408 on evidence. Make sure your student can differentiate between the different types of evidence she may see.

4. Give your student 3 minutes to complete the first two practice questions on page 409. Discuss the answers together.

5. Cover the material on pages 410-414 on organization and reasoning. Make sure your student understands how to track an argument throughout a passage using the "Deadbeat Dams" sample passage.

6. Give your student 5 minutes to answer the practice questions on page 414. Discuss the answers together.

ESSAY PRACTICE (15 MINUTES)

1. Using the techniques you have just reviewed, read and analyze Essay Prompt #2 together with your student. Make sure your student makes notes regarding language use, evidence, and organization and reasoning.

2. Let your student take the lead on analyzing the passage, but support him or him as he or she does so and point out any interesting or important parts of the passage he or she overlooks. Your student will keep working with this prompt for homework.

HOMEWORK

At the end of your session, answer any questions and assign the homework:

Hours 11-12	
Assignment	Page(s)
Memorize prefixes 1-10 (to *extro*)	229
Memorize vocabulary words 81-100	233-234
All remaining questions from Passport to Advanced Math review	587-636
Passport to Advanced Math practice set	637-646
Complete essay outline for Prompt #2	440-441

SECTION 4
16-HOUR TUTORING CURRICULUM

The 16-hour tutoring curriculum consists of the following curriculum pages built on top of the previous 8- and 12-hour tutoring outlines. To complete the full 16-hour tutoring curriculum, first work through hours 1-8 from the 8-hour outline and hours 9-12 from the 12-hour outline, and then continue with the following pages to work through hours 13-16.

Hours 13-14
Reading Question Types + Math Problem Solving

Task	Materials (All Pages in New SAT Guide)	Time
Homework Review	Pgs. 229; 233-234; 587-636; 637-646; 440-441	15 minutes
Understanding the Facts questions	Pgs. 108-142	60 minutes
Problem Solving and Data Analysis	Pgs. 647-722	45 minutes

Homework Review (15 minutes)

1. Use this time to review any questions or exercises that your student had trouble with, or to quiz your student on what strategies or information he or she read about in the New SAT Guide.

2. This time should also include vocabulary review, where you quiz your student on the roots, prefixes, and suffixes previously assigned for homework, along with words from the vocabulary list.

Understanding the Facts Questions (60 minutes)

1. Cover the material on pages 108-111 on Information and Ideas questions, and the first type, Words and Phrases in Context questions. Make sure your student understands that he or she is looking for a synonym of the word in question, and the strategies for reaching the answer.

2. Give your student 3 minutes to complete the practice questions on page 111-112. Discuss the answers using the answer key on page 114.

3. Cover the material on pages 115-118 on explicit and implicit meaning questions. Make sure your student understands the difference between the two question types,

and the question wording that indicates an implicit meaning question, as discussed on page 117.

4. Give your student 8 minutes to read the passage and complete the practice questions on pages 119-120. Discuss how your student marked up his or her passage, and then discuss the answers using the answer key on page 122.

5. Cover the material on pages 123-127 on central ideas and relationships questions. Make sure your student understands the difference between the two question types, and the importance of referring back to the passage to answer them both.

6. Give your student 5 minutes to read the passage and complete the practice questions on page 127-128. Discuss how your student marked up his or her passage, and then discuss the answers using the answer key on page 130.

7. Cover the material on pages 131-134 on evidence questions. Make sure your student understands how these questions will be paired with another, previous question as discussed on page 131.

8. Give your student 8 minutes to read the passage and complete the practice questions on pages 134-135. Discuss the answers using the answer key on page 136.

9. Cover the material on pages 137-138 on analogical reasoning. Make sure your student understands what an analogy is, as discussed in page 137.

10. Give your student 5 minutes to complete the practice questions on pages 139-140. Discuss the answers using the answer key on page 142.

PROBLEM SOLVING AND DATA ANALYSIS (45 MINUTES)

1. Cover the material on pages 647-722 on problem solving and data analysis concepts as needed, based on what topics your student struggles with. Make sure your student understands measurements and units; properties of data; ratios, rates, and proportions; statistics and probability; modeling data; and using data as evidence.

2.   Work through a few practice questions in each topic to gauge your student's understanding. The remaining practice questions can be assigned for homework.

HOMEWORK

At the end of your session, answer any questions and assign the homework:

Hours 13-14	
Assignment	Page(s)
Memorize prefixes 11-20 (to *post*)	229-230
Understanding the Facts practice set	143-150
All remaining questions from Problem Solving and Data Analysis review	647-722
Problem Solving and Data Analysis practice set	723-734

HOURS 15-16

Task	Materials *(All Pages in New SAT Guide)*	Time
Homework Review	Pgs. 229-230; 143-150; 647-722; 723-734	15 minutes
Grammar Review	Pgs. 283-324; Common Grammar Errors worksheet; Confused Words & Idioms quiz;	15 minutes
Grammar practice set	Pgs. 327-332	30 minutes
Essay practice	Pgs. 442-443	60 minutes

HOMEWORK REVIEW (15 MINUTES)

1. Use this time to review any questions or exercises that your student had trouble with, or to quiz your student on what strategies or information he or she read about in the New SAT Guide.

2. This time should also include vocabulary review, where you quiz your student on the roots, prefixes, and suffixes previously assigned for homework, along with words from the vocabulary list.

GRAMMAR REVIEW

1. Review key grammar concepts with your student, focusing on the concepts he or she struggles with the most. Your student should be comfortable with all the material covered on pages 283-324.

2. You can also give your student the Common Grammar Errors worksheet, or the Confused Words & Idioms quiz. You can modify or adapt the quiz to suit the needs of your student. Give your student 5 minutes to complete each worksheet. Discuss the answers together using the Teacher Answer Key.

GRAMMAR PRACTICE SET (30 MINUTES)

1. Give your student 12 minutes to complete the first 15 questions in the practice set on pages 327-332. For each question, have your student select his or her answer and also identify the category of error. For example, question #1 has an error with subjects and objects; the object "me" is used instead of the subject "I." Discuss the answers and the category of error using the answer key on page 334.

2. Give your student another 12 minutes complete the remaining questions, again identifying the category of error for each one. Discuss the answers and the category of error using the answer key on page 334.

ESSAY PRACTICE (60 MINUTES)

1. Give your student 5 minutes to read and analyze Essay Prompt #3 on pages 442-443. Make sure your student considers or marks up how the author uses language, evidence, and organization and reasoning to make his or her argument. Discuss these elements together.

2. Your student will now work on drafting an essay in parts. Pause to discuss each portion after it is written.

3. Give your student 5 minutes to brainstorm further and write an essay introduction in response to the prompt.

4. Discuss the introduction together. Make sure that your student has included a clear thesis that briefly mentions his or her supporting arguments.

5. Give your student 12 minutes to write the essay's first body paragraph.

6. Discuss the body paragraph together, asking for your student to describe the point of his or her paragraph. Make sure that your student has included a topic sentence, three to four supporting sentences, and a concluding sentence. You can also make sure that your student has used appropriate transitions between his or her sentences.

7. Give your student 10 minutes to write his or her next body paragraph.

8. Discuss the body paragraph together, asking for your student to describe the point of his or her paragraph. Make sure that your student has included a topic sentence, three to four supporting sentences, and a concluding sentence. You can also make sure that your student has used appropriate transitions between his or her sentences.

9. You will likely not have enough time for your student to write a third body paragraph. Instead, ask your student what her third body paragraph would discuss, or have your student complete it for homework.

10. Give your student 5 minutes to write his or her conclusion.

11. Discuss the conclusion together. Make sure that your student has included a topic sentence, three to four supporting sentences, and a concluding sentence. You can also double-check that your student has not added in any new information in his or her conclusion.

HOMEWORK

At the end of your session, answer any questions and assign the homework:

Hours 15-16	
Assignment	Page(s)
Memorize final 8 prefixes	230
Memorize words 101-120	234-235
Reading Practice Section timed	240-252
Math Practice Section timed	822-827

Section 5
20-hour Tutoring Curriculum

The 20-hour tutoring curriculum consists of the following curriculum pages built on top of the previous 8-, 12-, and 16-hour tutoring outlines. To complete the full 20-hour tutoring curriculum, first work through hours 1-16 from those outlines, and then continue with the following pages to work through hours 17-20.

HOURS 17-18
READING QUESTION TYPES + ADDITIONAL TOPICS IN MATH

Task	Materials (All Pages in New SAT Guide)	Time
Homework Review	Pgs. 230; 234-235; 240-252; 822-827	15 minutes
Persuasive Language questions	Pgs. 152-180	45 minutes
Additional Topics in Math	Pgs. 735-796	60 minutes

HOMEWORK REVIEW (15 MINUTES)

1. Use this time to review any questions or exercises that your student had trouble with, or to quiz your student on what strategies or information he or she read about in the New SAT Guide.

2. This time should also include vocabulary review, where you quiz your student on the roots, prefixes, and suffixes previously assigned for homework, along with words from the vocabulary list.

PERSUASIVE LANGUAGE QUESTIONS (45 MINUTES)

1. Cover the material on pages 152-156 on the Persuasive Language category of questions, and Analyzing Word Choice questions. Make sure your student recalls rhetorical devices, and understands the tone words on page 155.

2. Give your student 5 minutes to complete the practice questions on pages 156-157. Discuss the answers using the answer key on page 158.

3. Cover the material on pages 159-162 on Analyzing Text Structure questions. Make sure your student understands how to mark up the structure of a passage, as shown on page 162.

4. Give your student 5 minutes to read and mark up the practice passage, and complete the questions on pages 162-163. Discuss the answers using the answer key on page 164.

5. Cover the material on pages 165-167 on Point of View and Purpose questions. Make sure your student understands the difference between the two question types.

6. Give your student 5 minutes to complete the practice questions on page 168. Discuss the answers using the answer key on page 170.

7. Cover the material on pages 171-176 on Analyzing Arguments questions. Make sure your student understands the definition of a counterclaim, and different types of evidence, as explained in the chart on page 173.

8. Give your student 8 minutes to read and mark up the practice passage and complete the questions on page 176-178. Discuss the answers using the answer key on page 180.

Additional Topics (60 minutes)

1. Cover the material on pages 735-796 on additional topics in math as needed, based on what topics your student struggles with. Make sure your student understands introductory geometry, right triangles, radians and degrees, circles, and complex numbers.

2. Work through a few practice questions in each topic to gauge your student's understanding. The remaining practice questions can be assigned for homework.

HOMEWORK

At the end of your session, answer any questions and assign the homework:

Hours 17-18	
Assignment	Page(s)
Memorize first 10 suffixes (to *–ful)*	230
Memorize words 121-140	234-235
Persuasive Language practice set	181-188
All remaining questions from Additional Topics review	735-796
Additional Topics practice set	797-807

Hours 19-20

Writing & Essay Practice + Test Day Prep

Task	Materials (All Pages in New SAT Guide)	Time
Homework Review	Pgs. 230; 234-235; 181-188; 735-796; 797-807	15 minutes
Writing Practice Section	375-382; 384	45 minutes
Essay practice	444-445	30 minutes
Test day approach and review	24-26	30 minutes

Homework Review (15 minutes)

1. Use this time to review any questions or exercises that your student had trouble with, or to quiz your student on what strategies or information he or she read about in the New SAT Guide.

2. This time should also include vocabulary review, where you quiz your student on the roots, prefixes, and suffixes previously assigned for homework, along with words from the vocabulary list.

Writing Practice Section (45 minutes)

1. Give your student 35 minutes to complete the full writing practice section on pages 375-382. Then, discuss the answers using the answer key on page 384.

2. If you prefer, you can also have your student pause partway through to review questions and discuss any difficulties. You can also break up the section into smaller portions if your student has trouble getting through the full section.

ESSAY PRACTICE (30 MINUTES)

1. Give your student 5 minutes to read and analyze Essay Prompt #4 on pages 444-445. Make sure your student considers or marks up how the author uses language, evidence, and organization and reasoning to make his or her argument. Discuss these elements together.

2. Give your student 5 minutes to brainstorm further and write an essay introduction in response to the prompt.

3. Discuss the introduction together. Make sure that your student has included a clear thesis that briefly mentions its supporting arguments.

4. Give your student 12 minutes to write the essay's first body paragraph.

5. Discuss the body paragraph together, asking for your student to describe the point of the paragraph. Make sure that your student has included a topic sentence, 3-4 supporting sentences, and a concluding sentence. You can also make sure that your student has used appropriate transitions between sentences.

6. You can opt to have your student complete the rest of the essay for homework.

TEST DAY APPROACH AND REVIEW (30 MINUTES)

1. Using pages 24-26, discuss with your student what to expect on test day. Help your student make a plan for approaching test day, including what to review in the days leading up to the test, how to stay calm and focused, and what your student's approach will be for each section.

2. Also use this time to review any final questions with your student, and to go over important reminders and strategies for each section of the test based on your student's needs.

HOMEWORK

At the end of your session, answer any questions and assign the homework:

Hours 19-20	
Assignment	Page(s)
Memorize the remaining 10 suffixes	230
Memorize words 141-160	235-236
Complete the remainder of Sample Prompt #4 essay	444-445
Complete a 50-minute practice essay using Sample Prompt #5	446-447
Math practice section timed	809-818